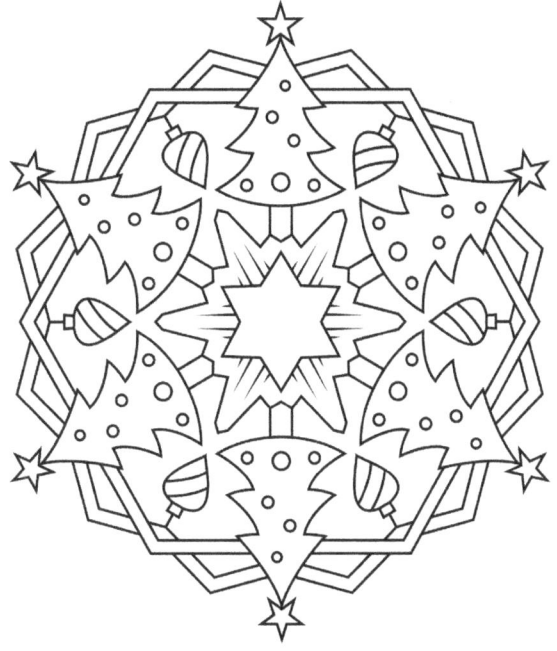

This Christmas Mandala Coloring Book Belongs To:

_____

_____

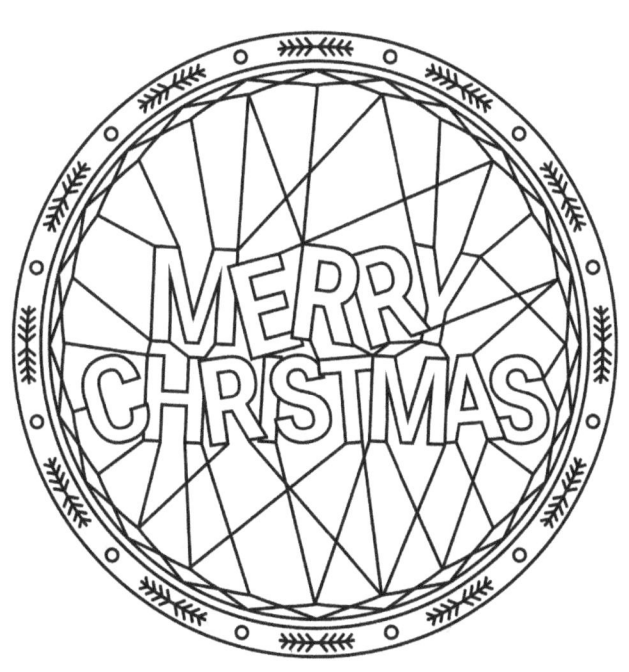

Copyright ©2020 Practical Journals and Planners All rights reserved.
No part of this book may be reproduced or transmitted in any form or by any means electronical or mechanical including photocopying, recording, scanning or any other information storage retrieval system without permission from the Publisher.
www.PracticalJournalsandPlanners.com

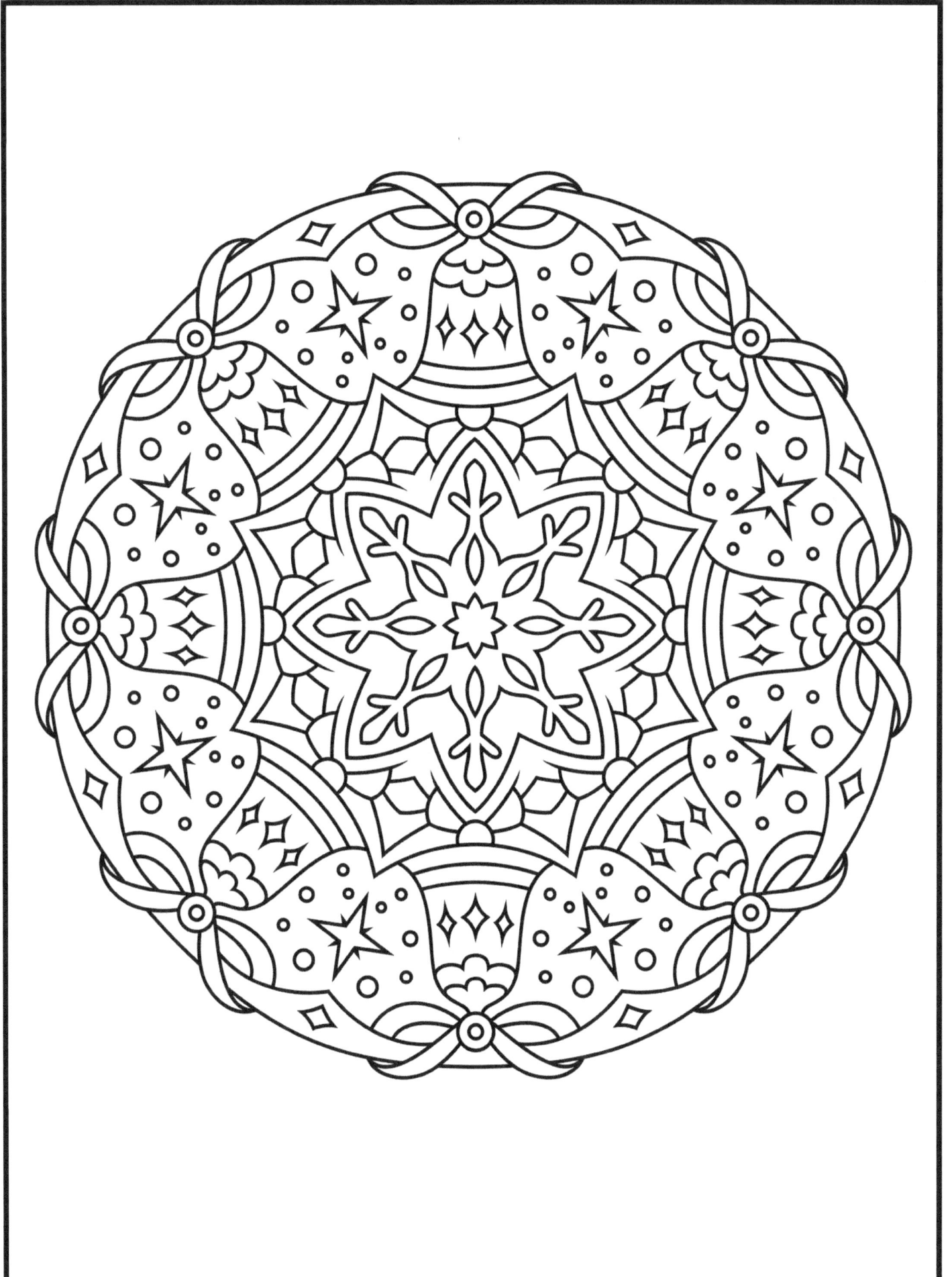

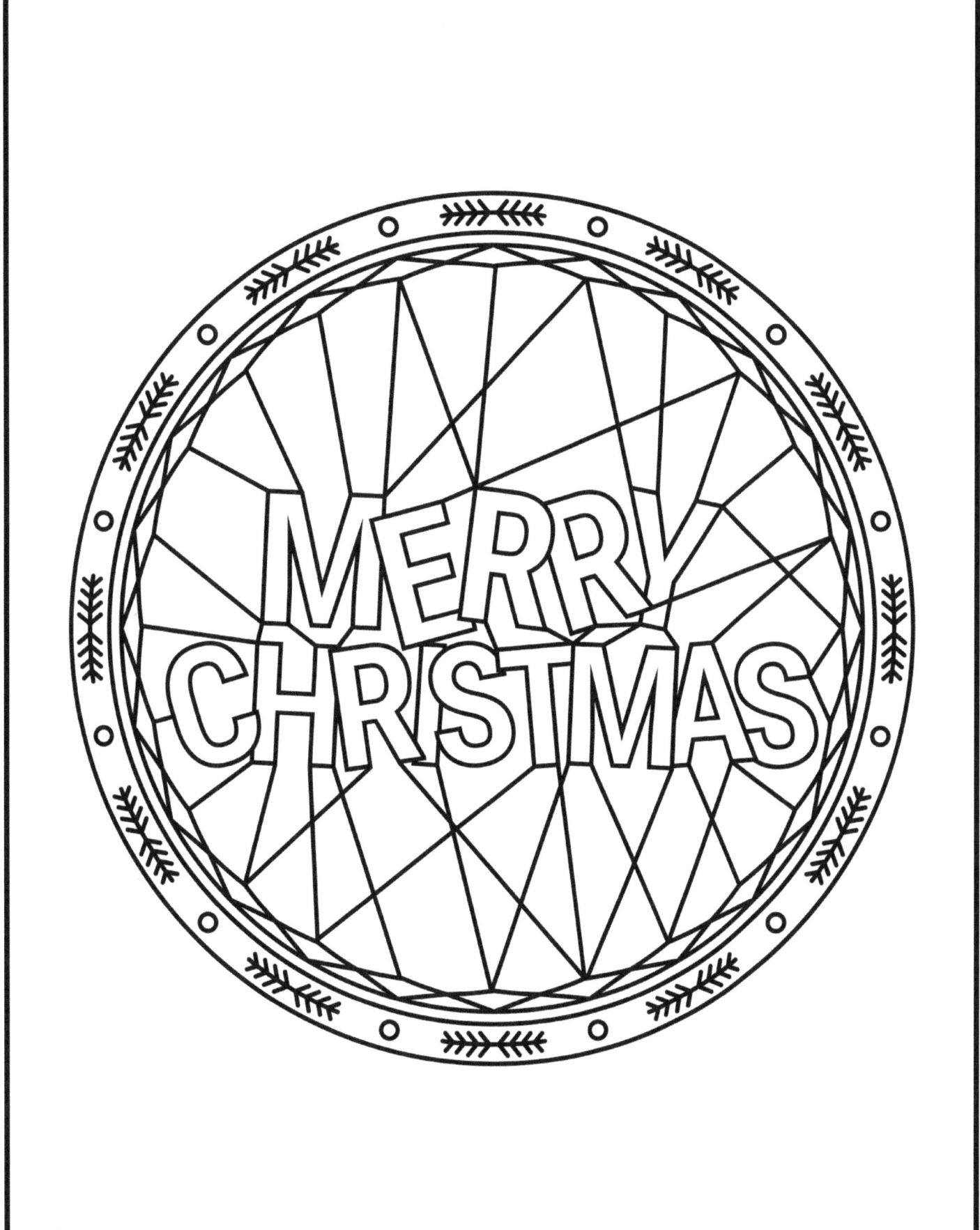

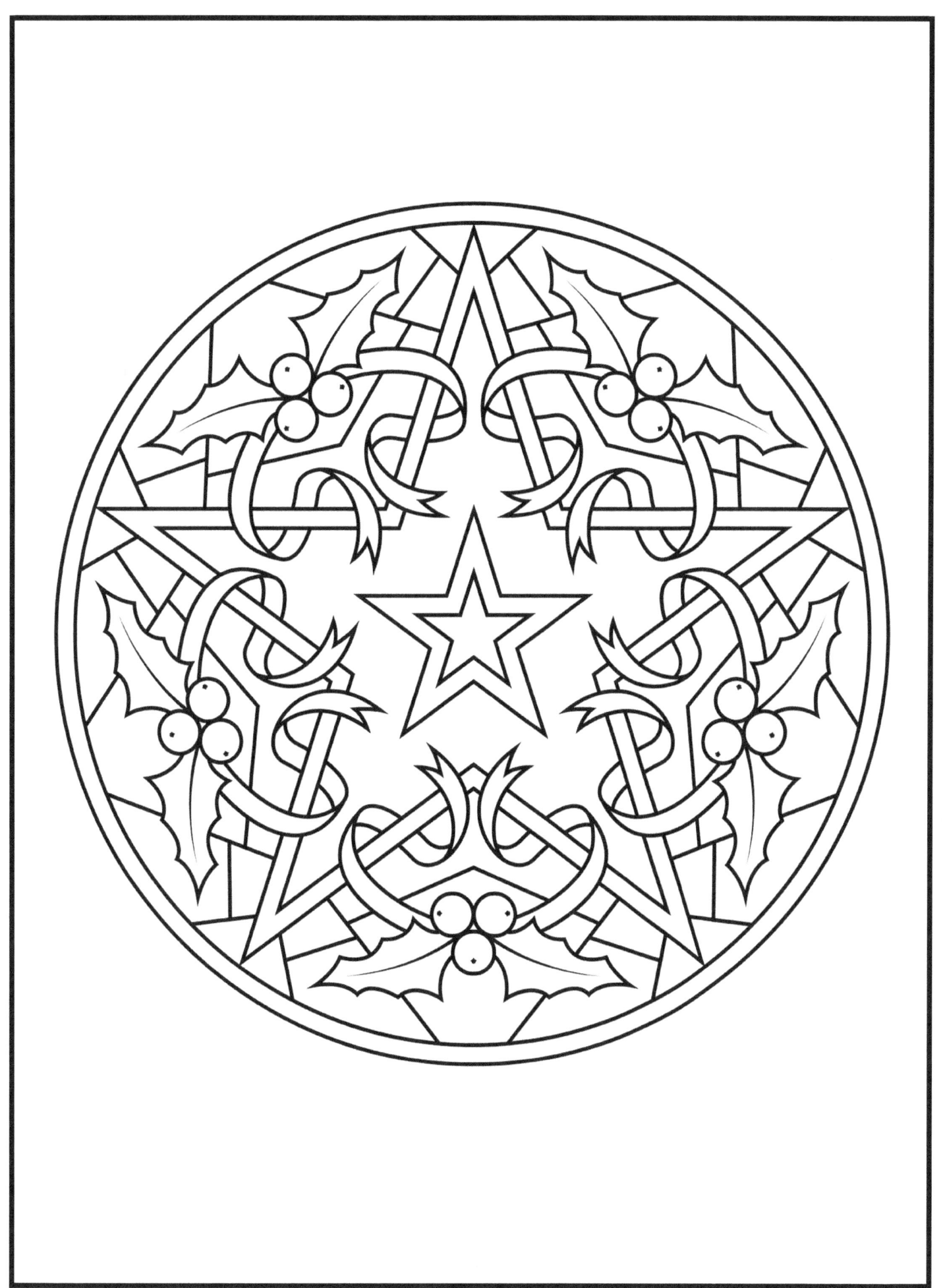

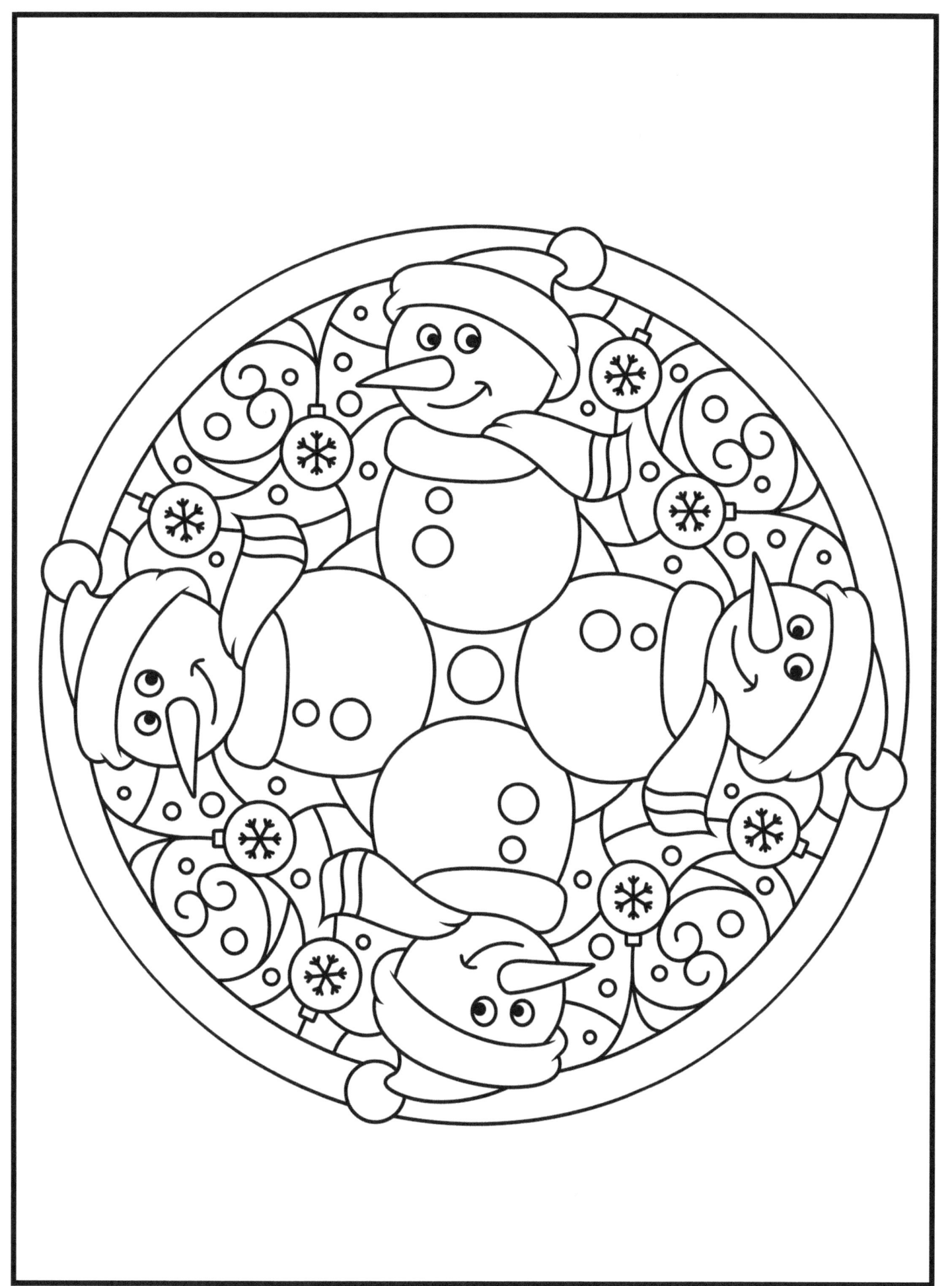

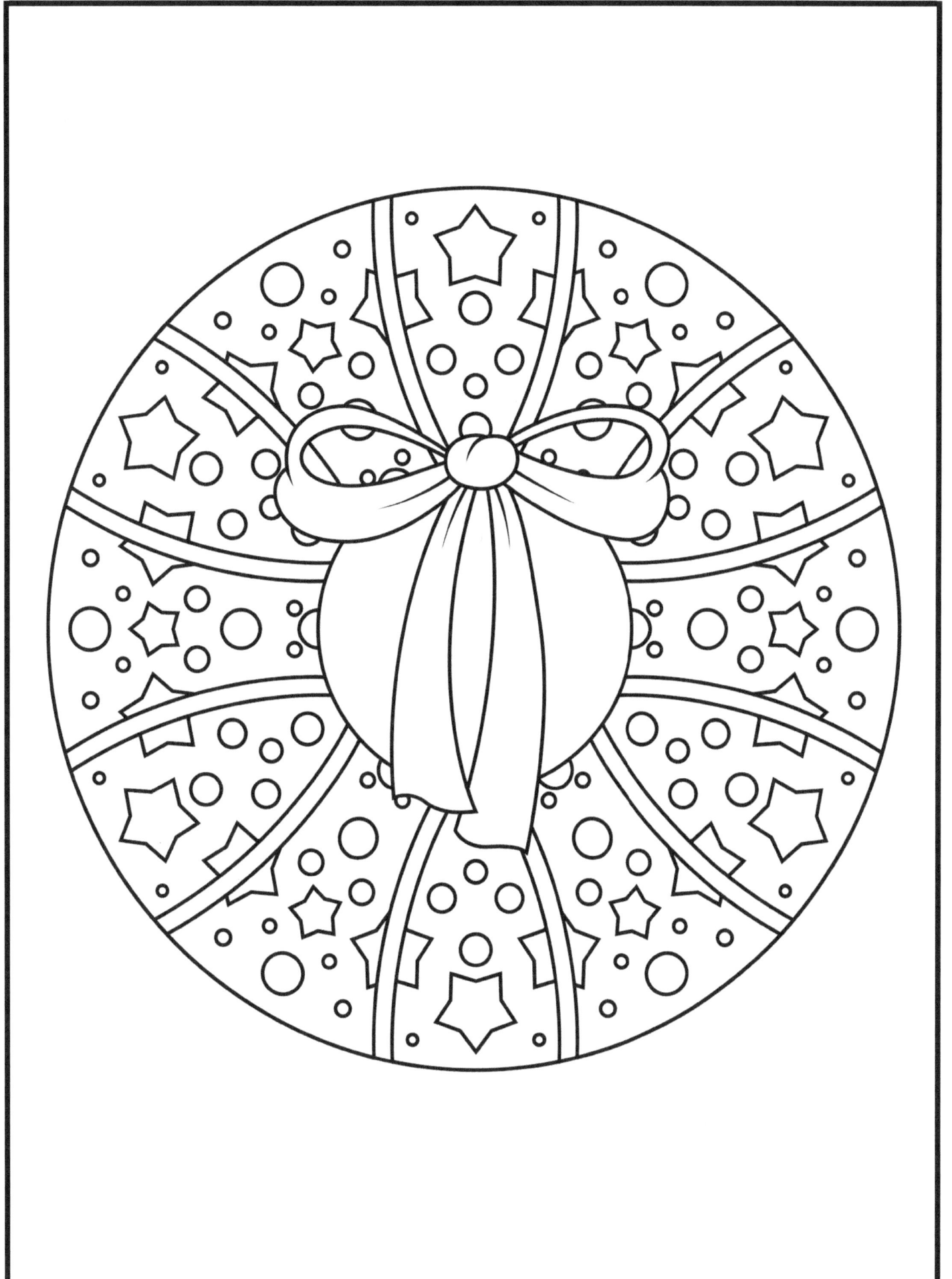

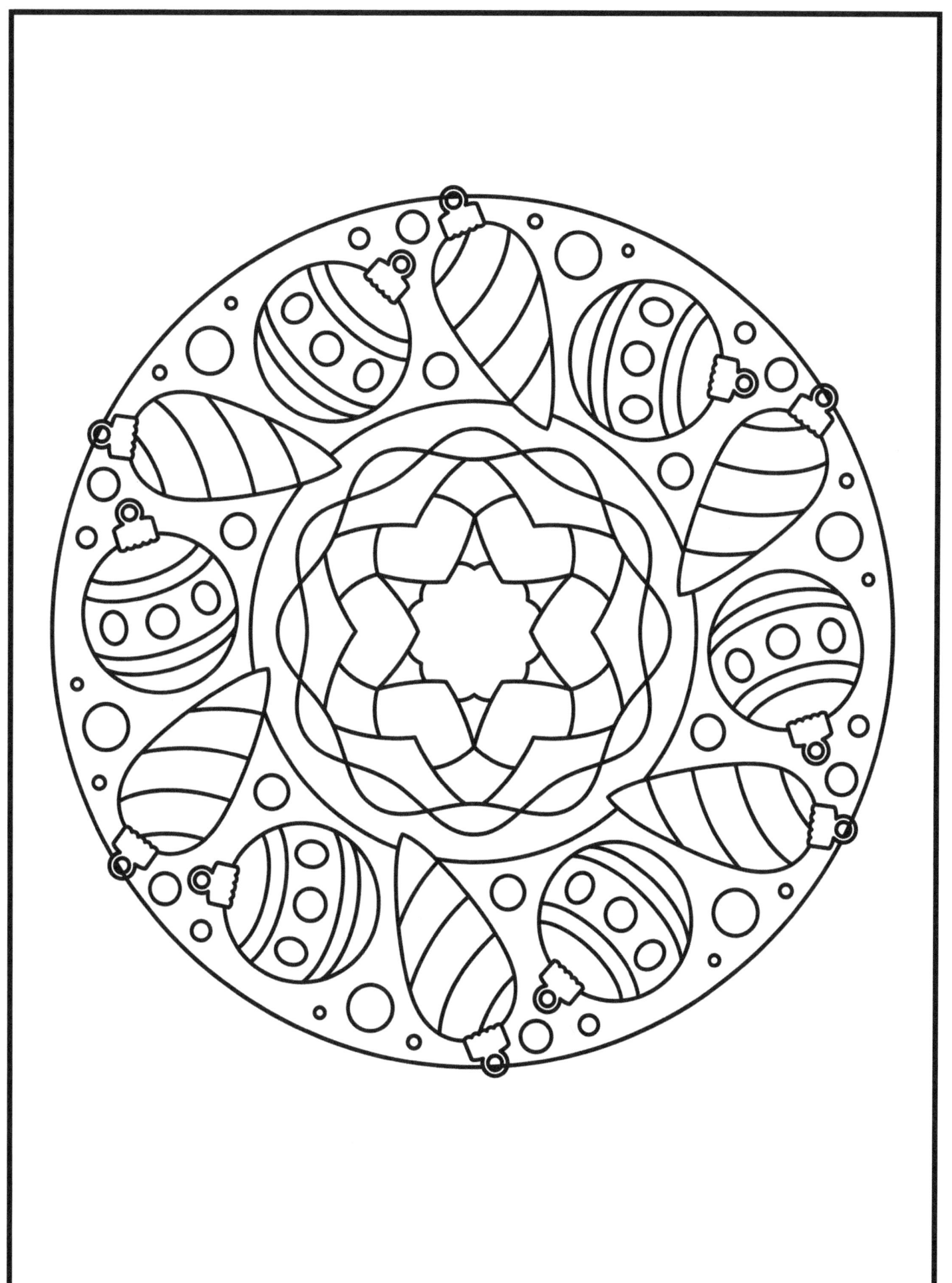

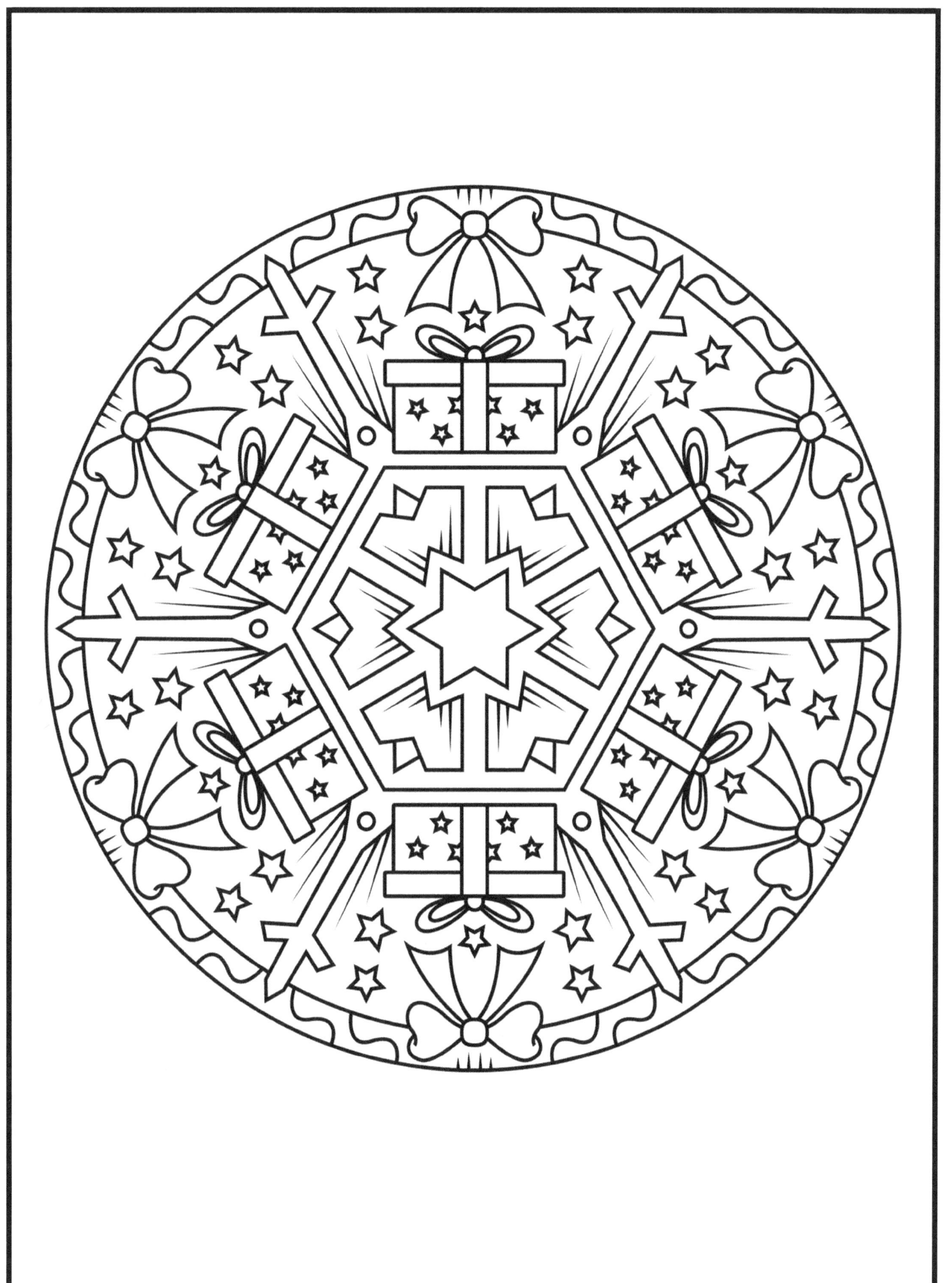

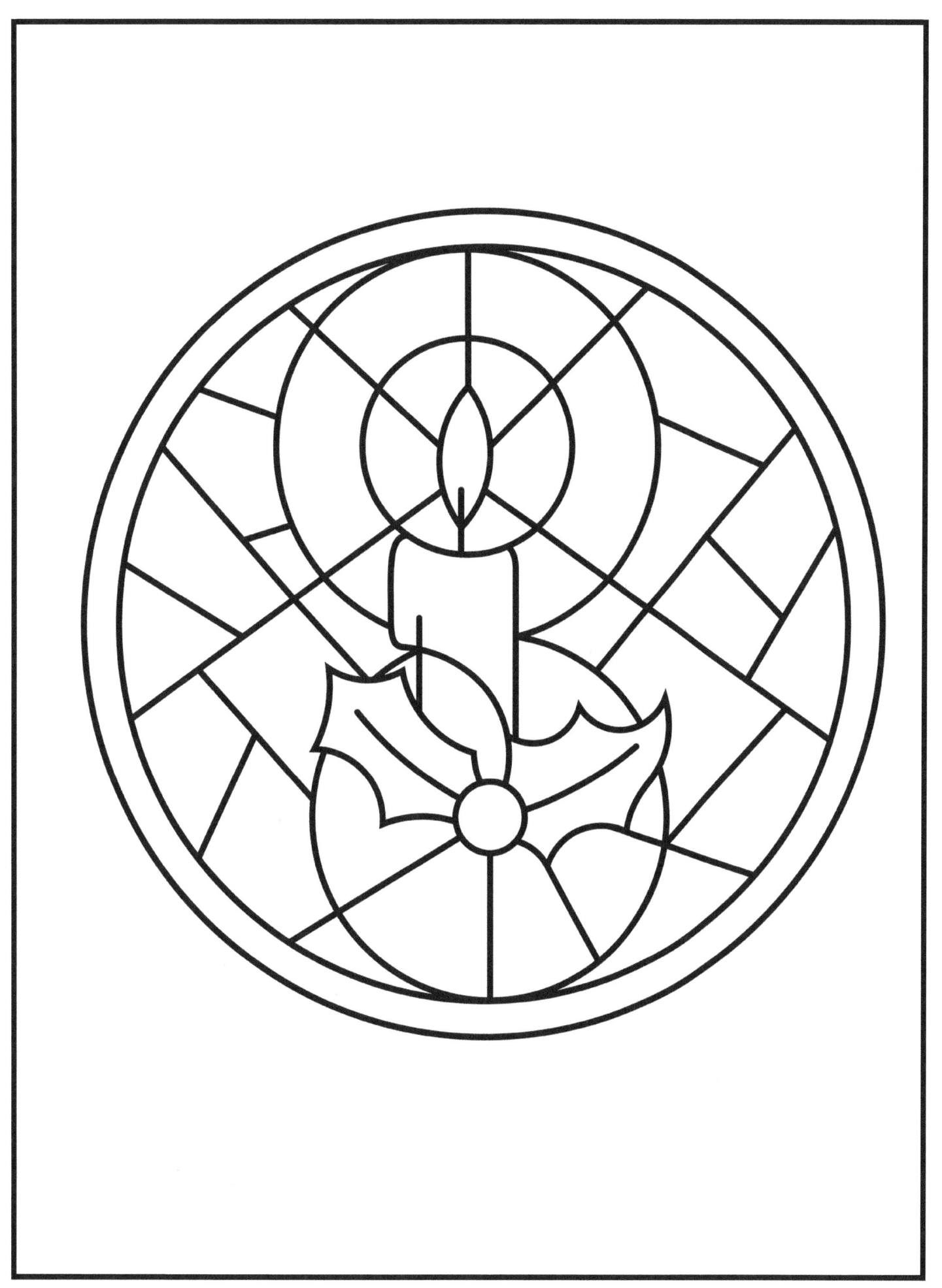

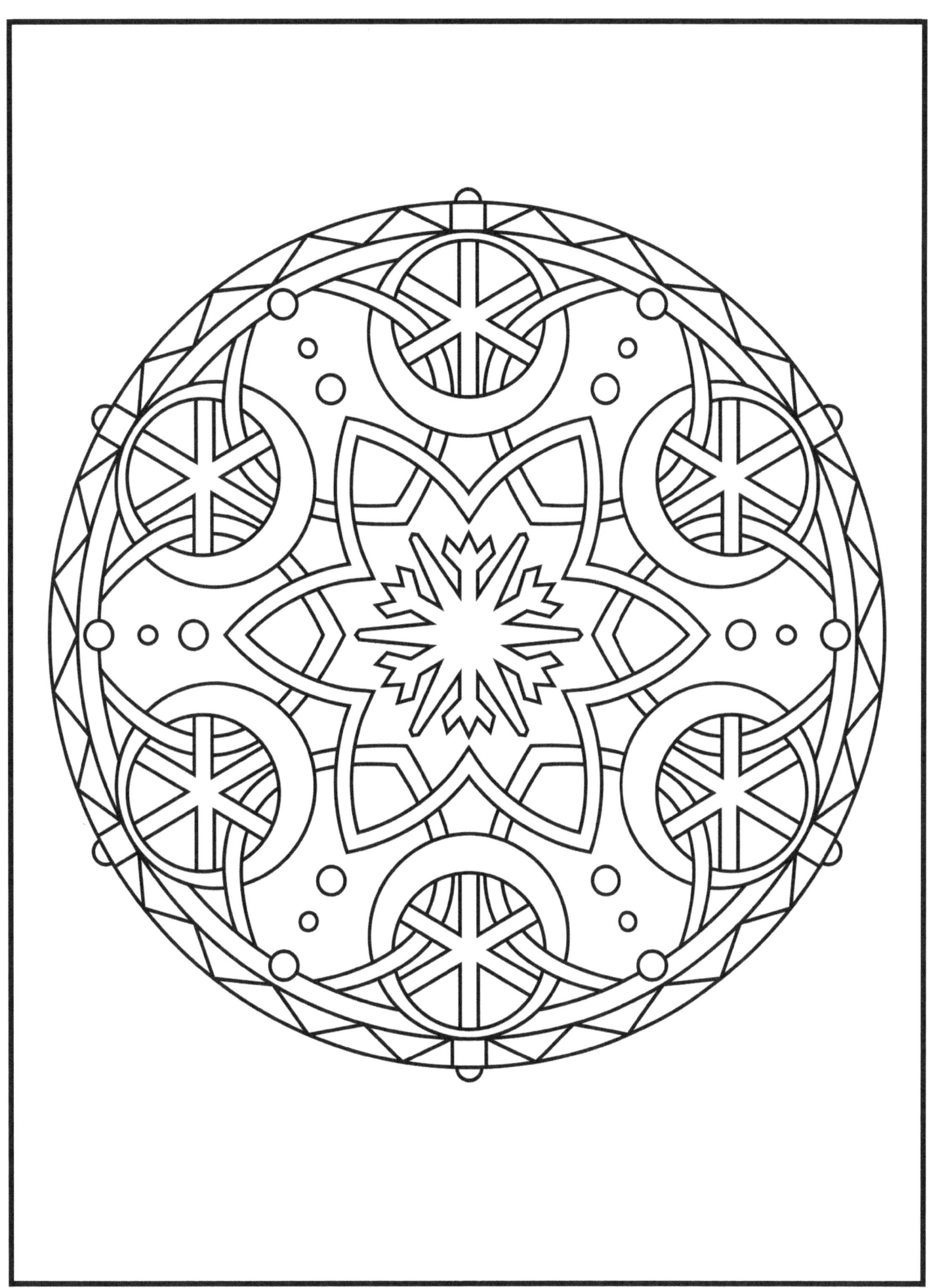

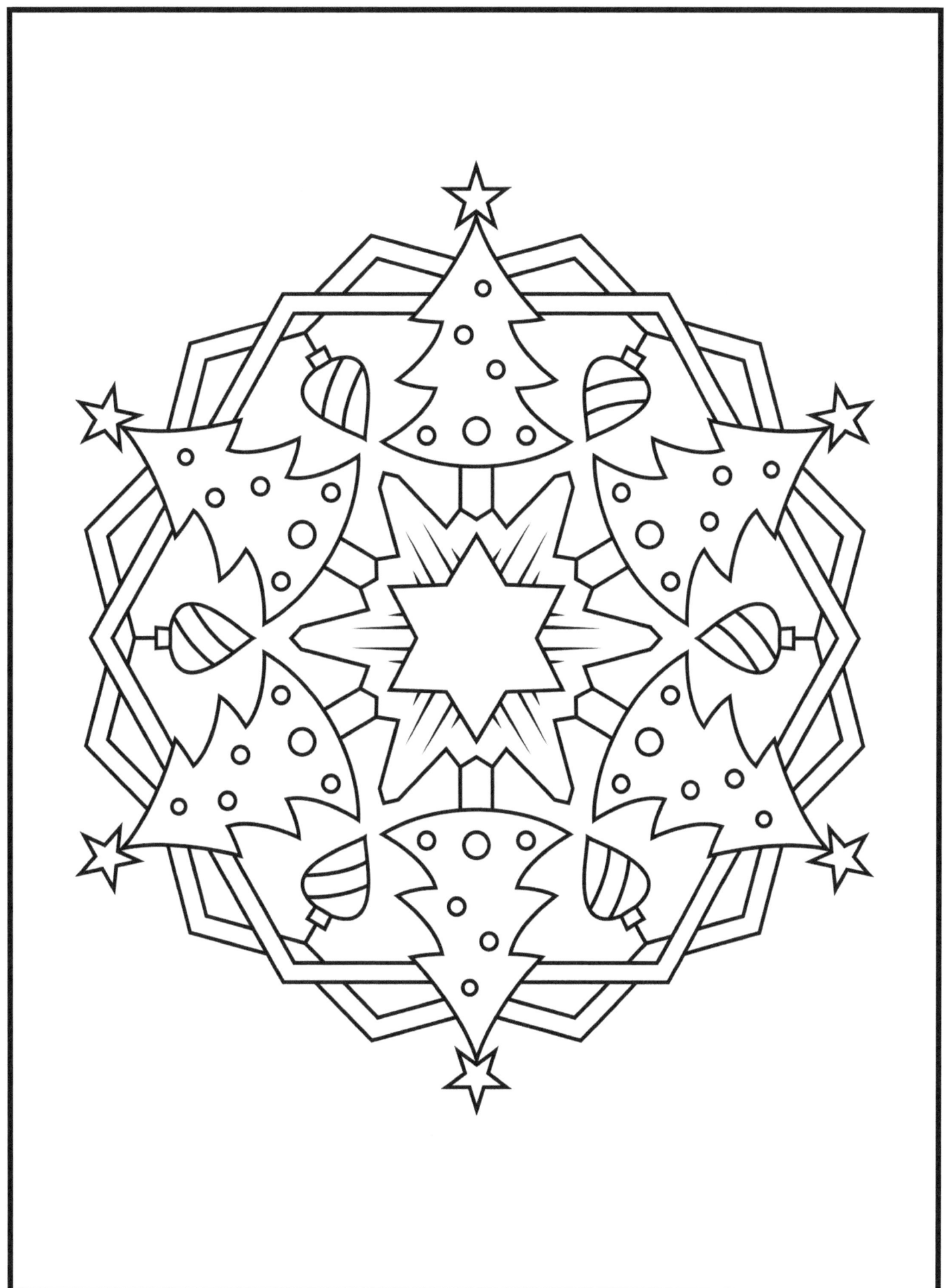

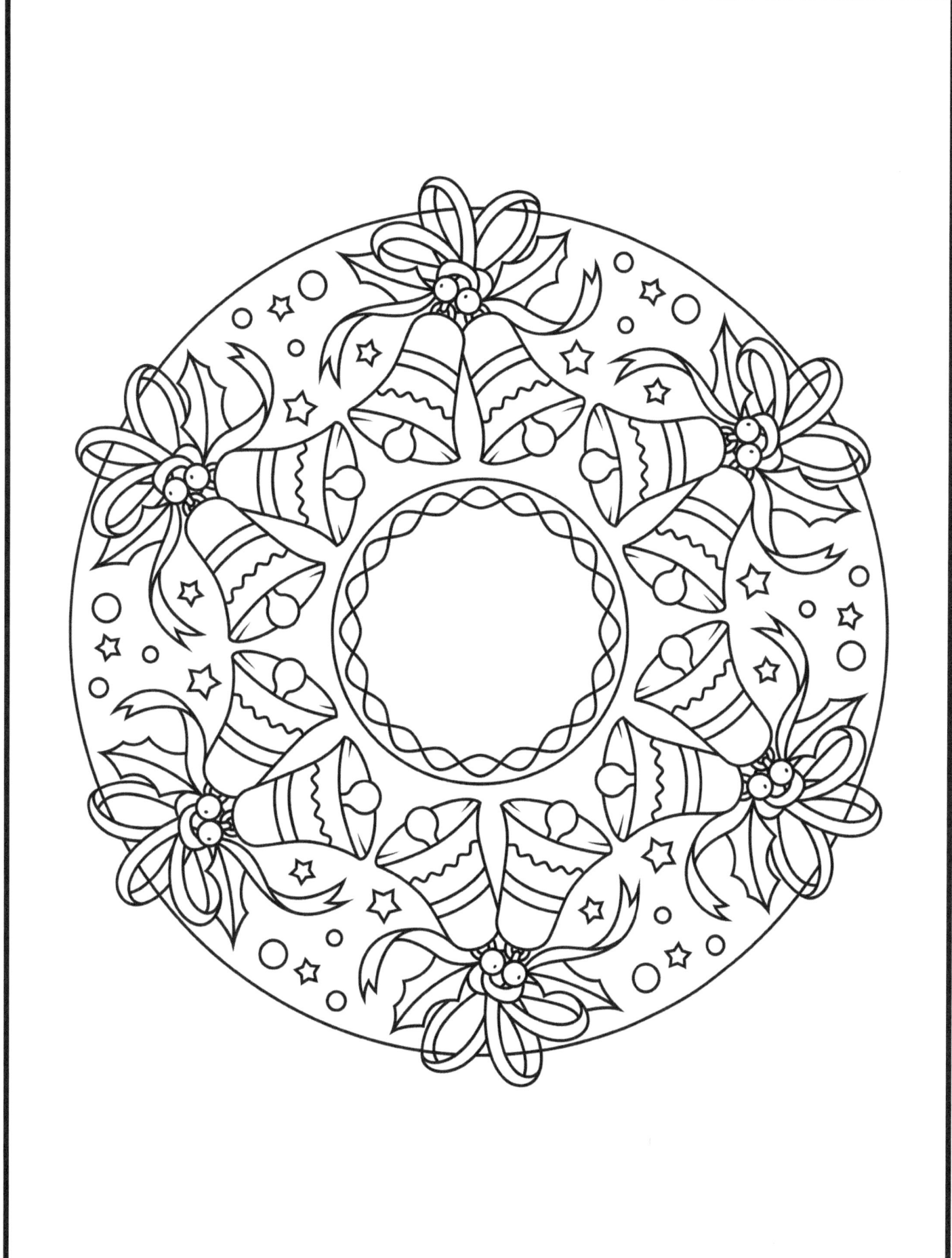

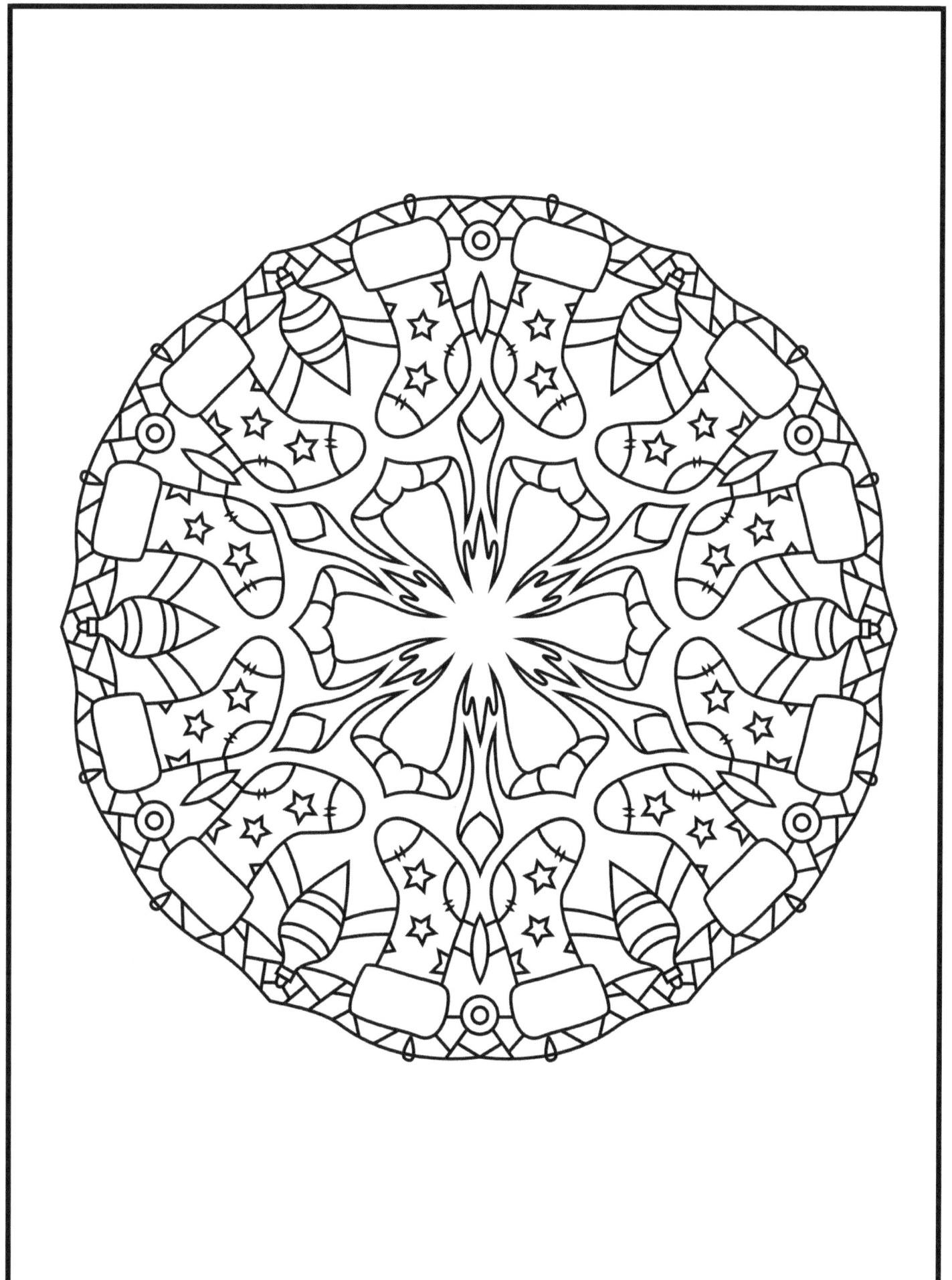

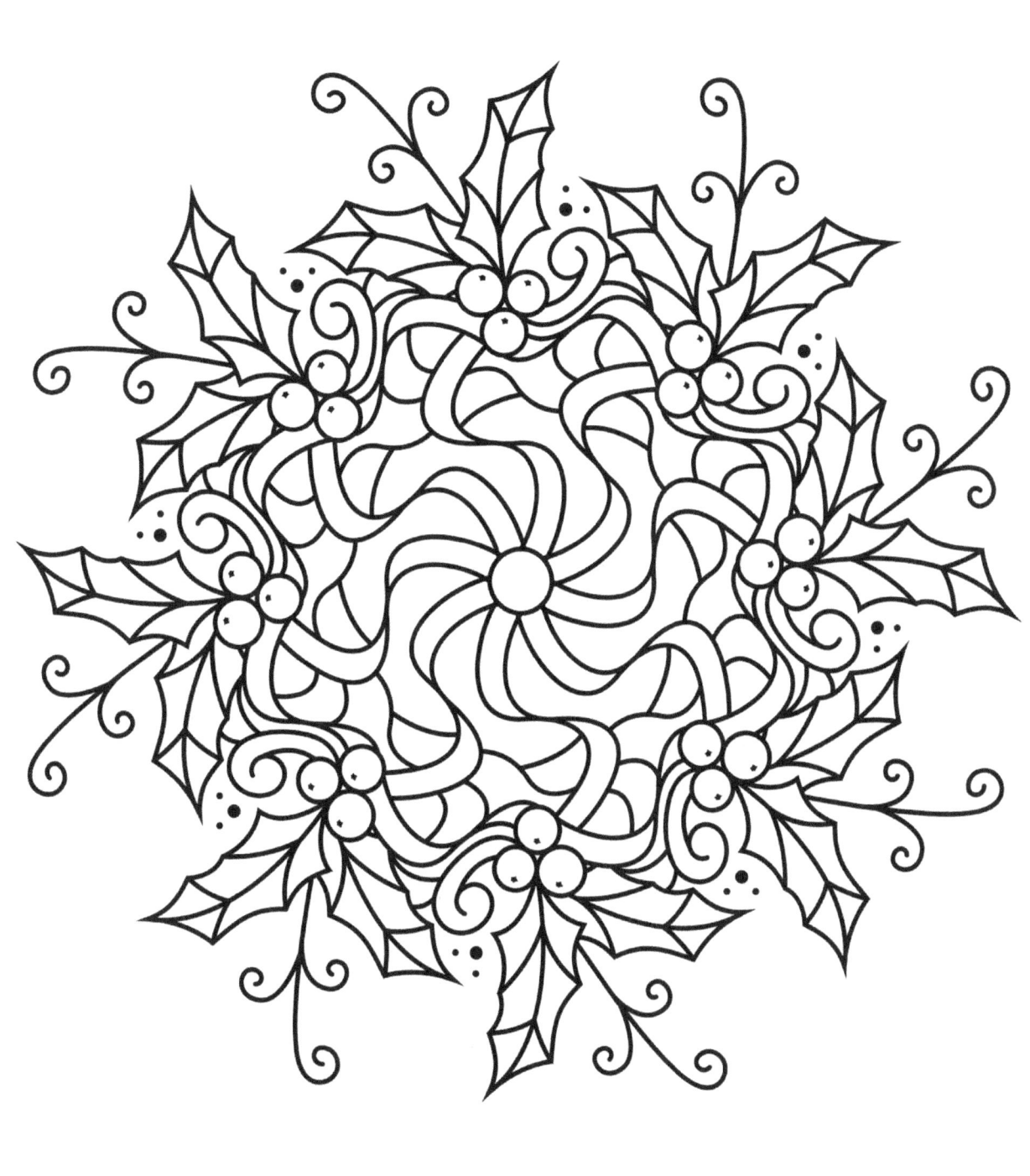

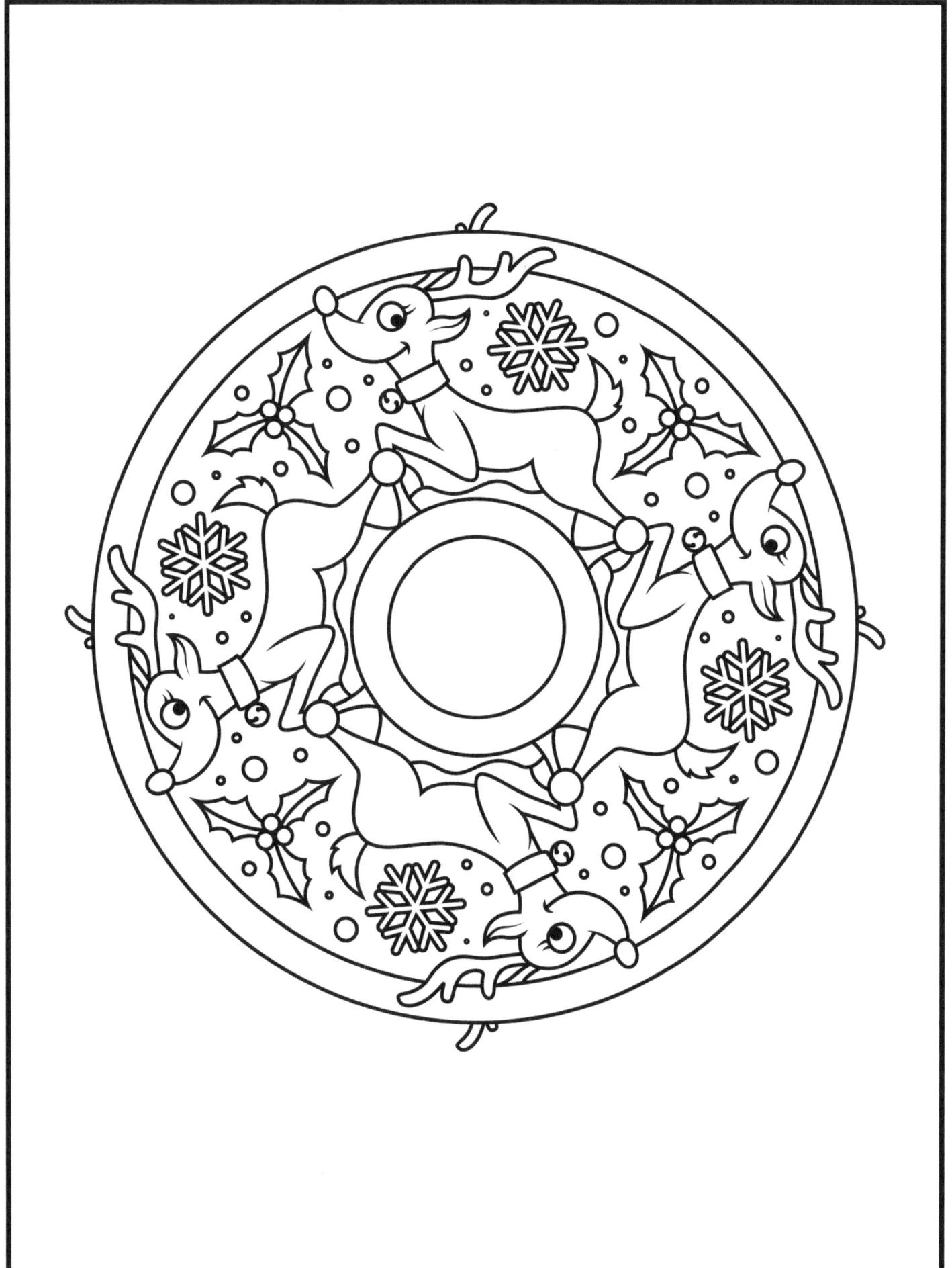

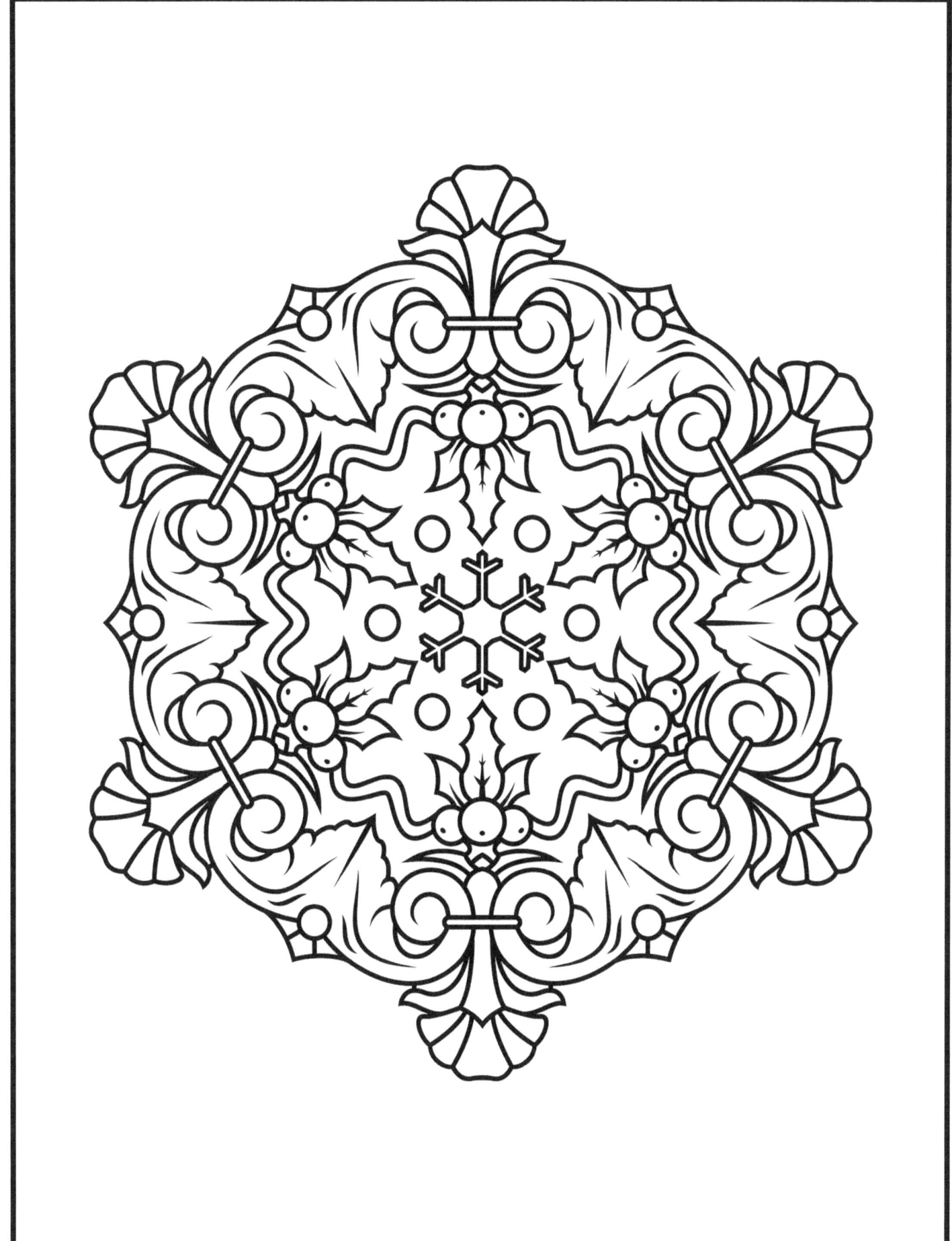

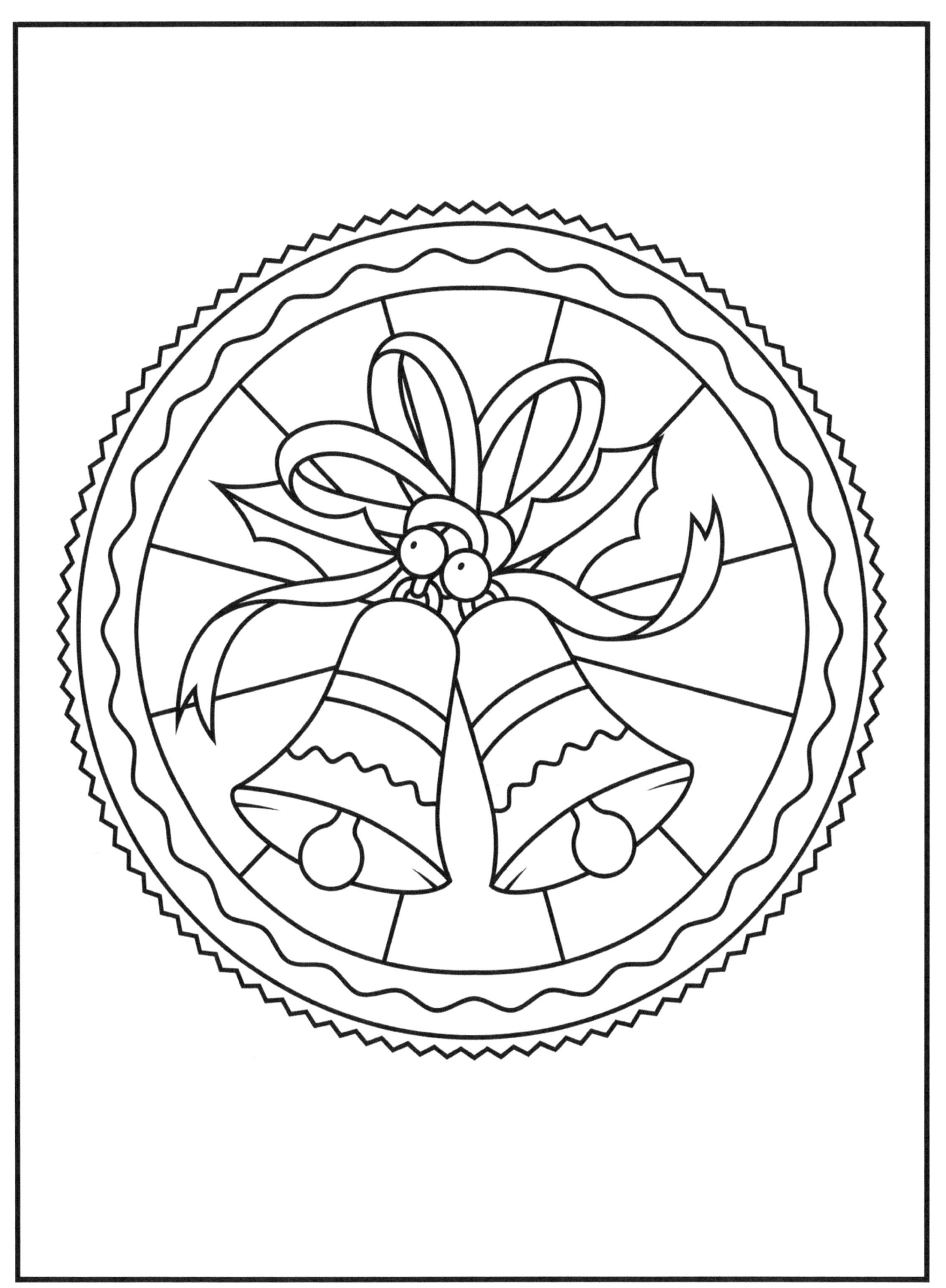

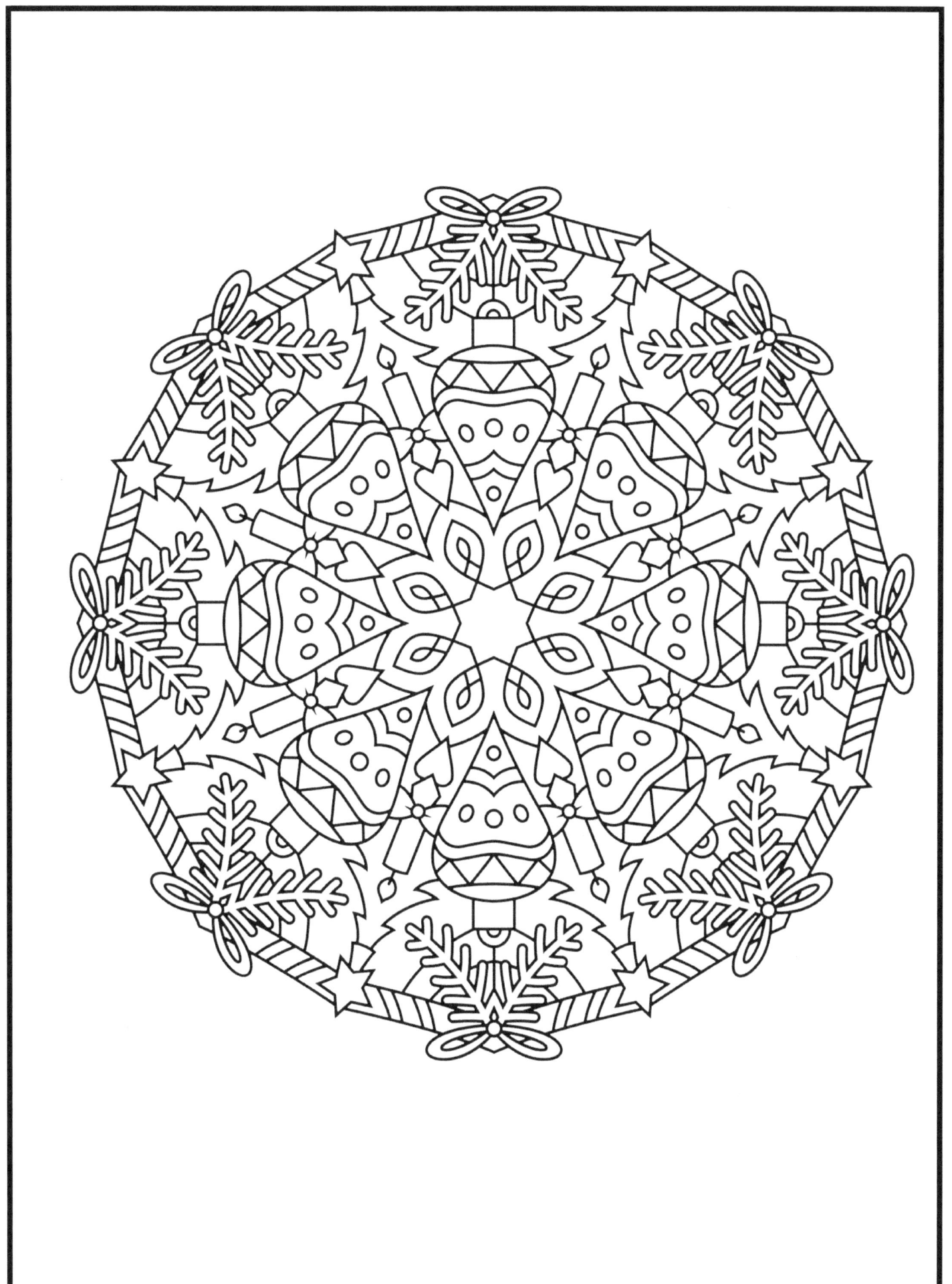

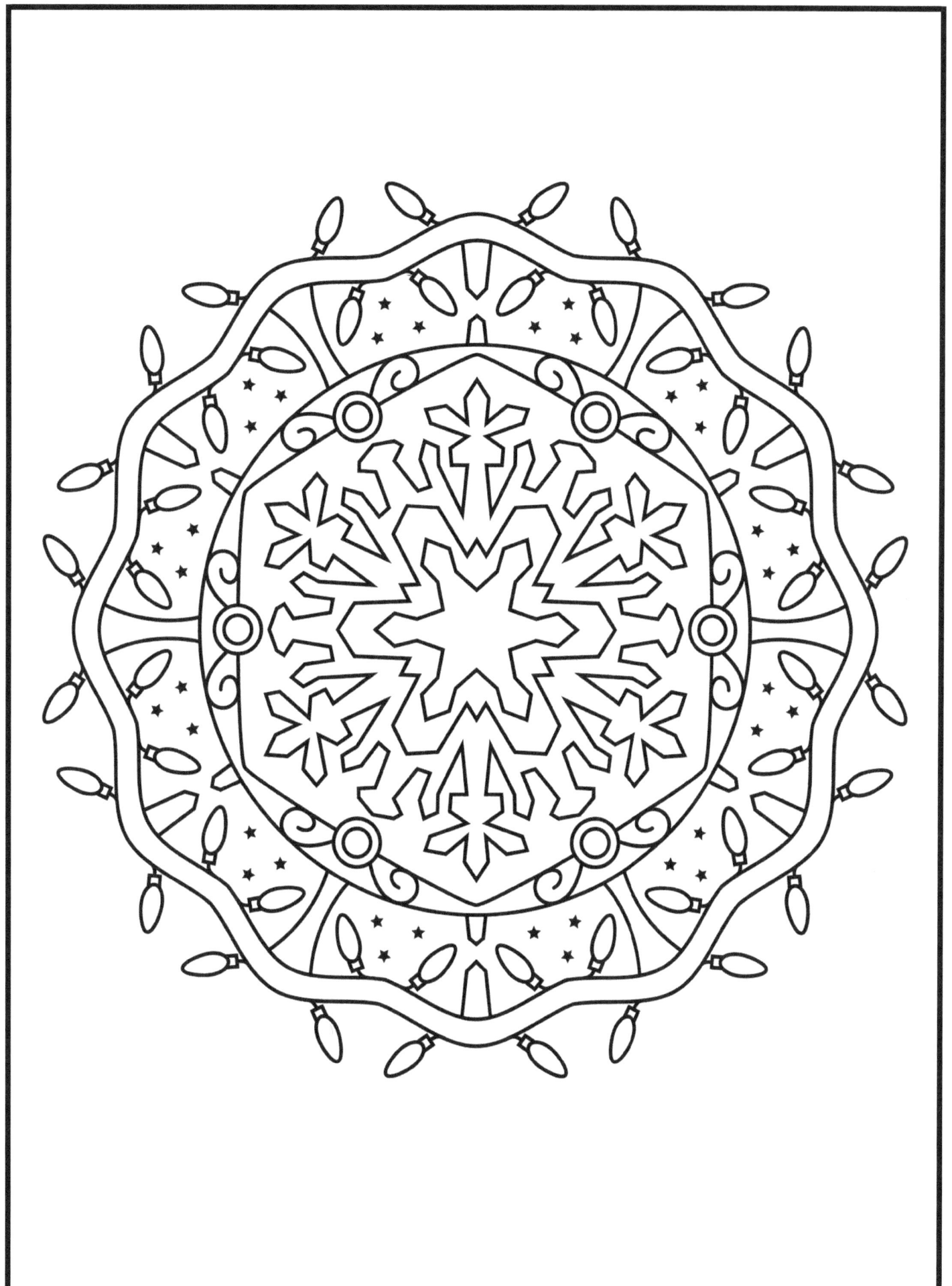

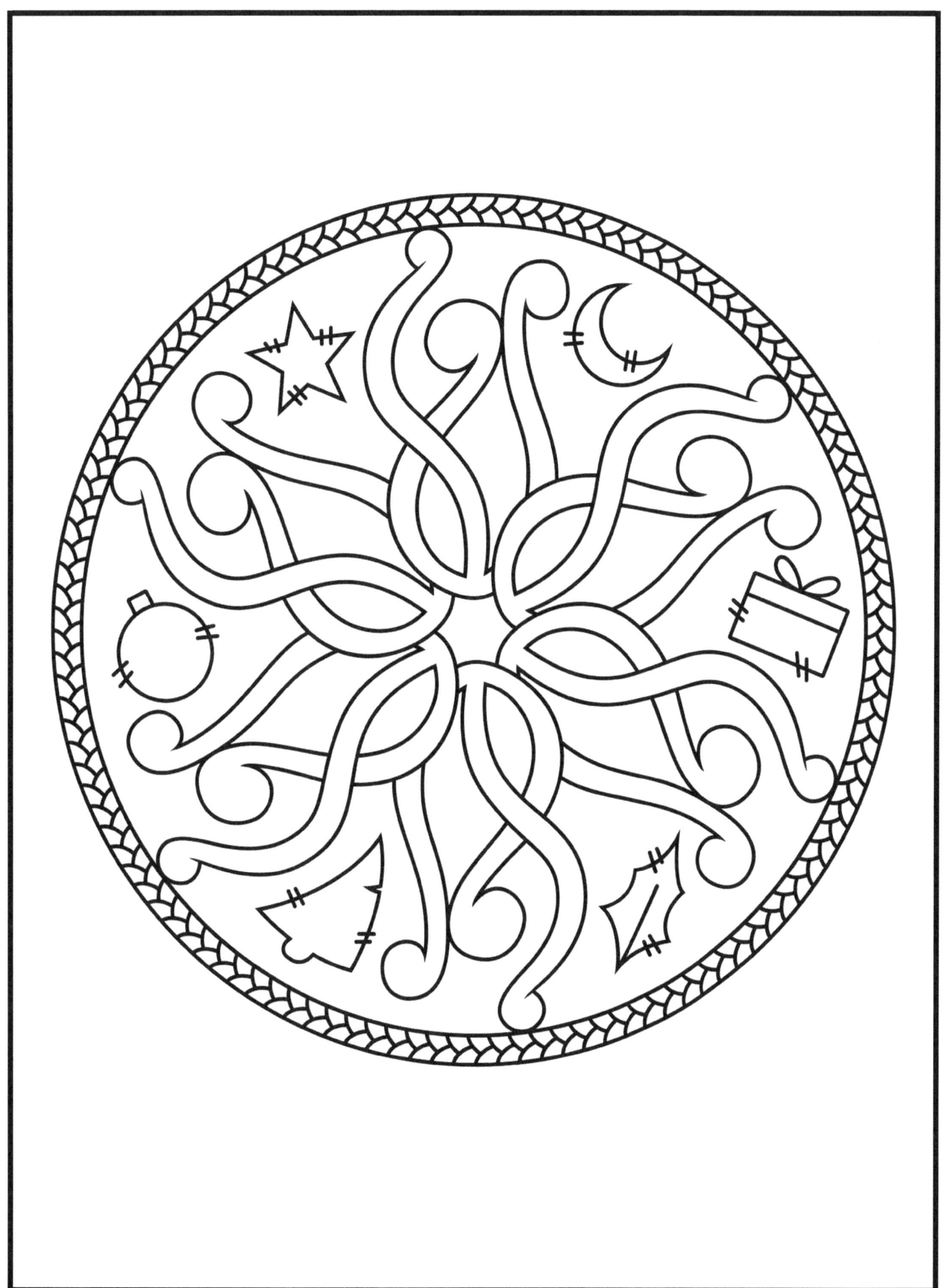

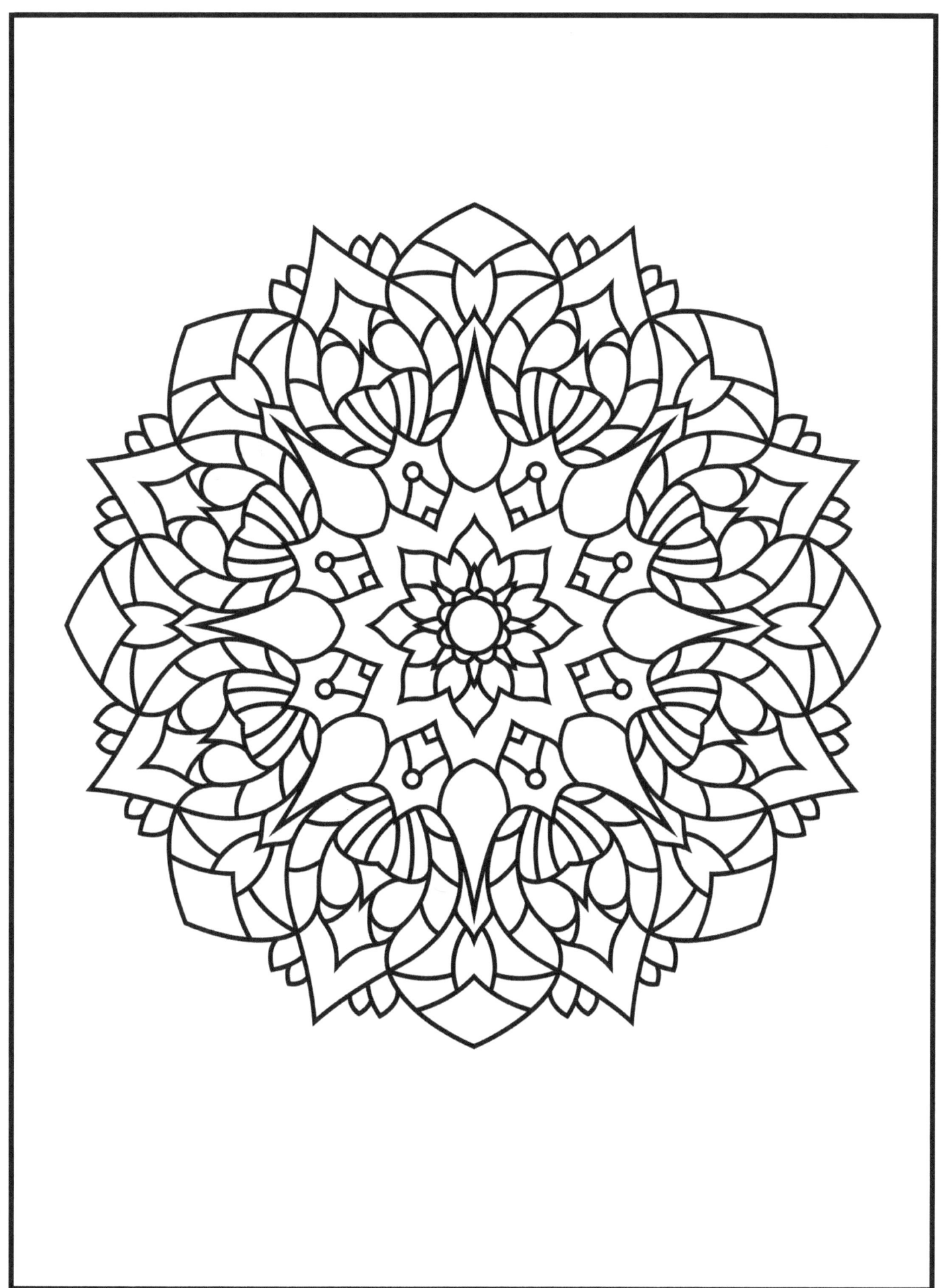

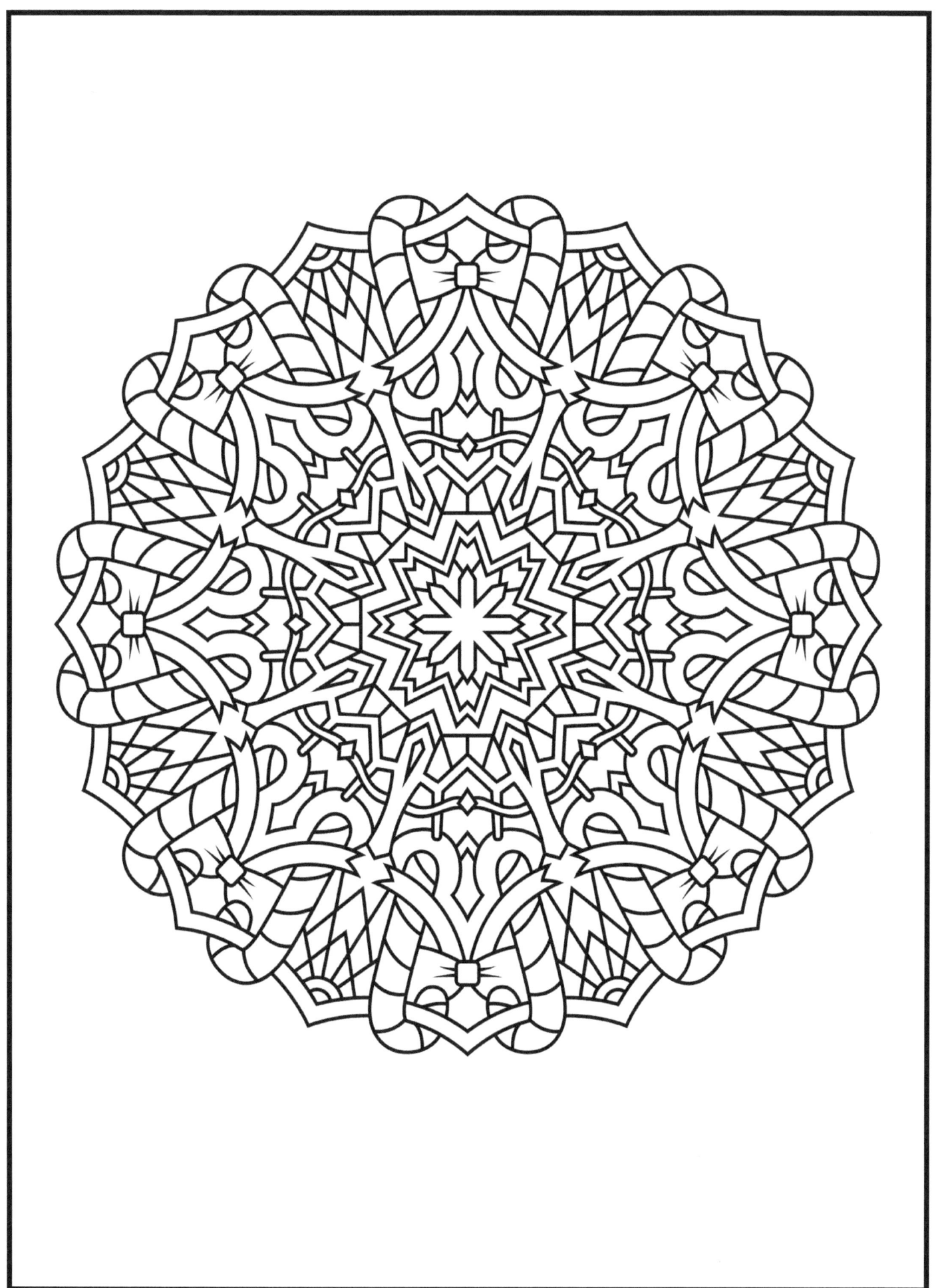

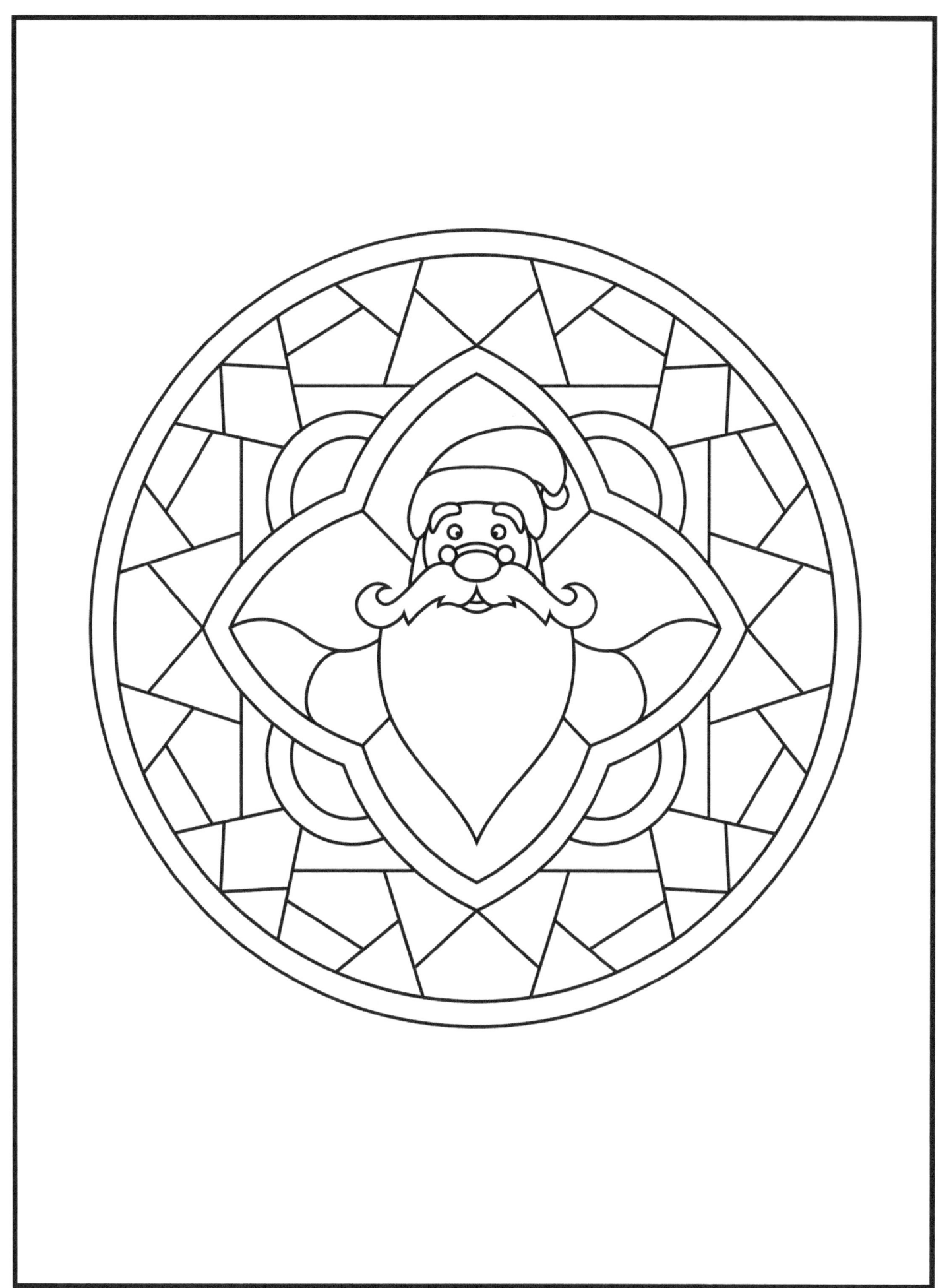

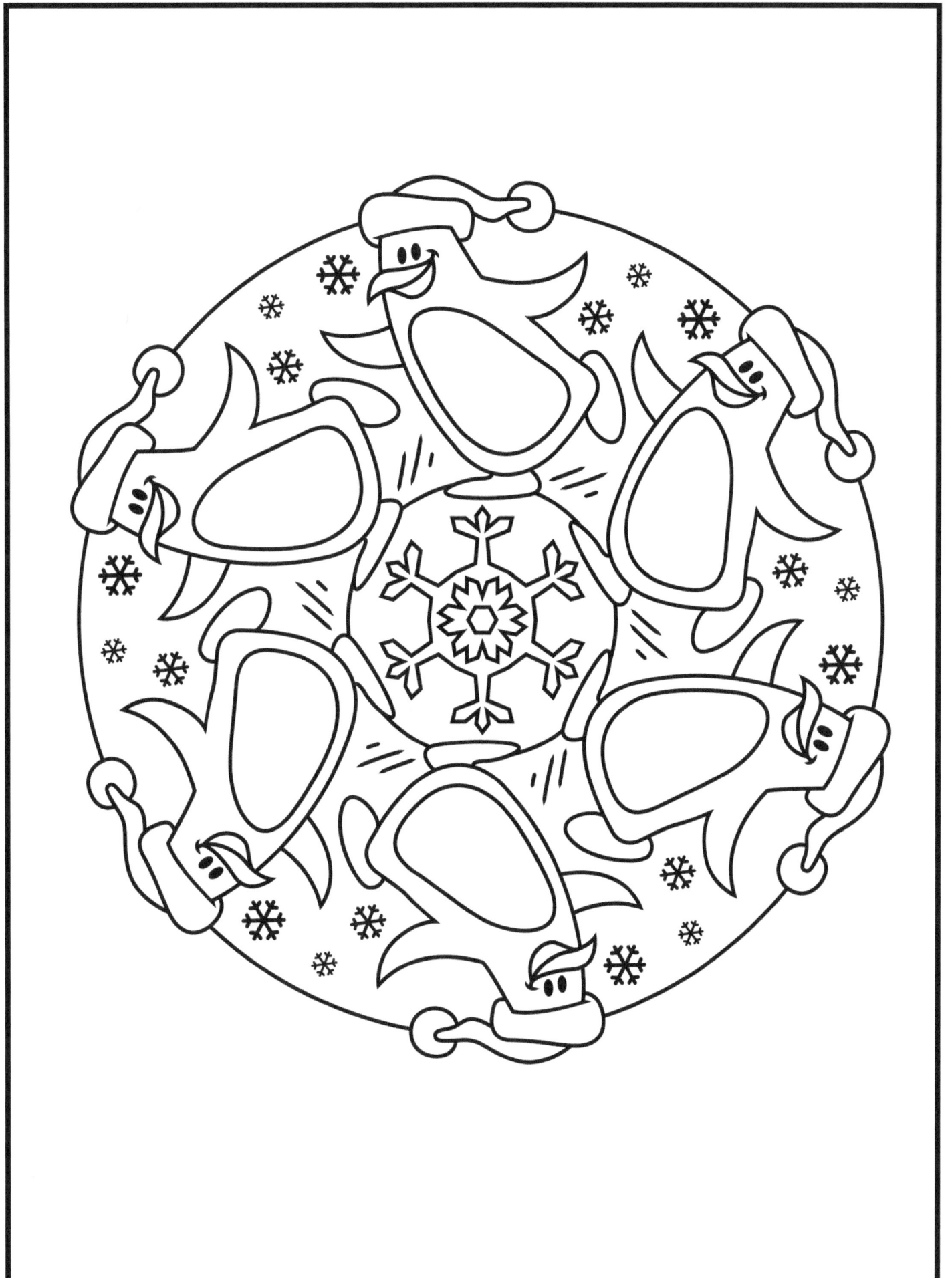

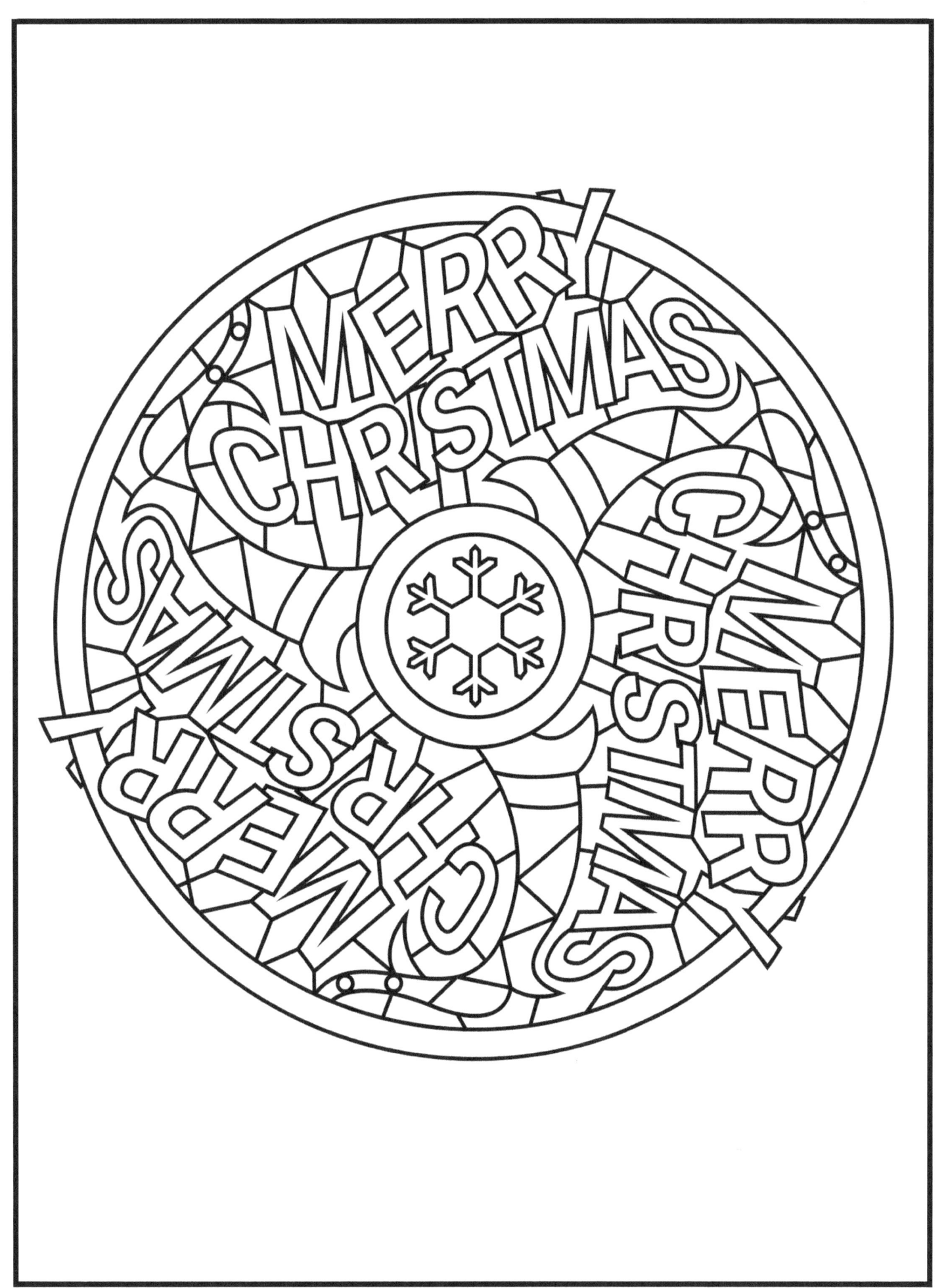

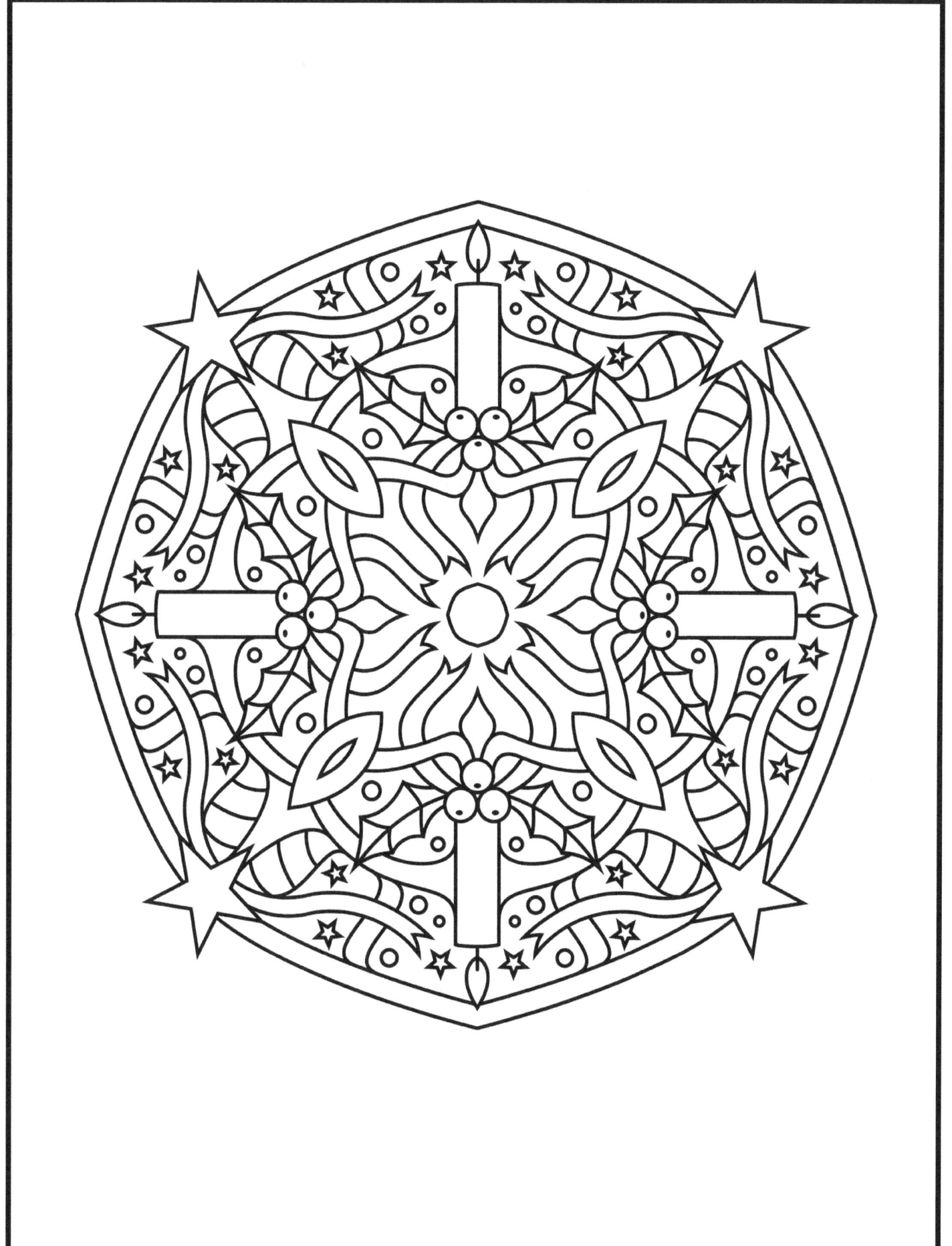

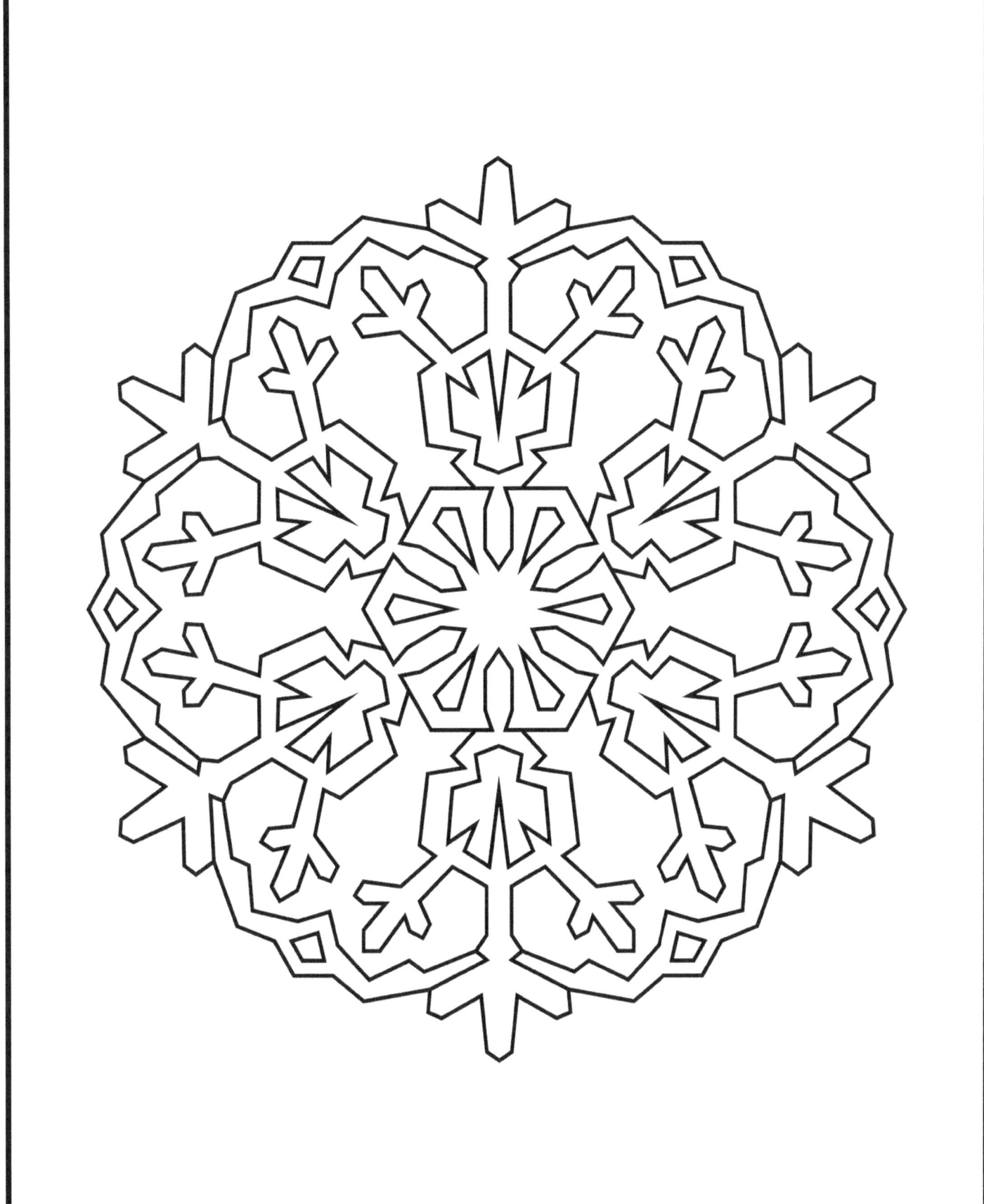

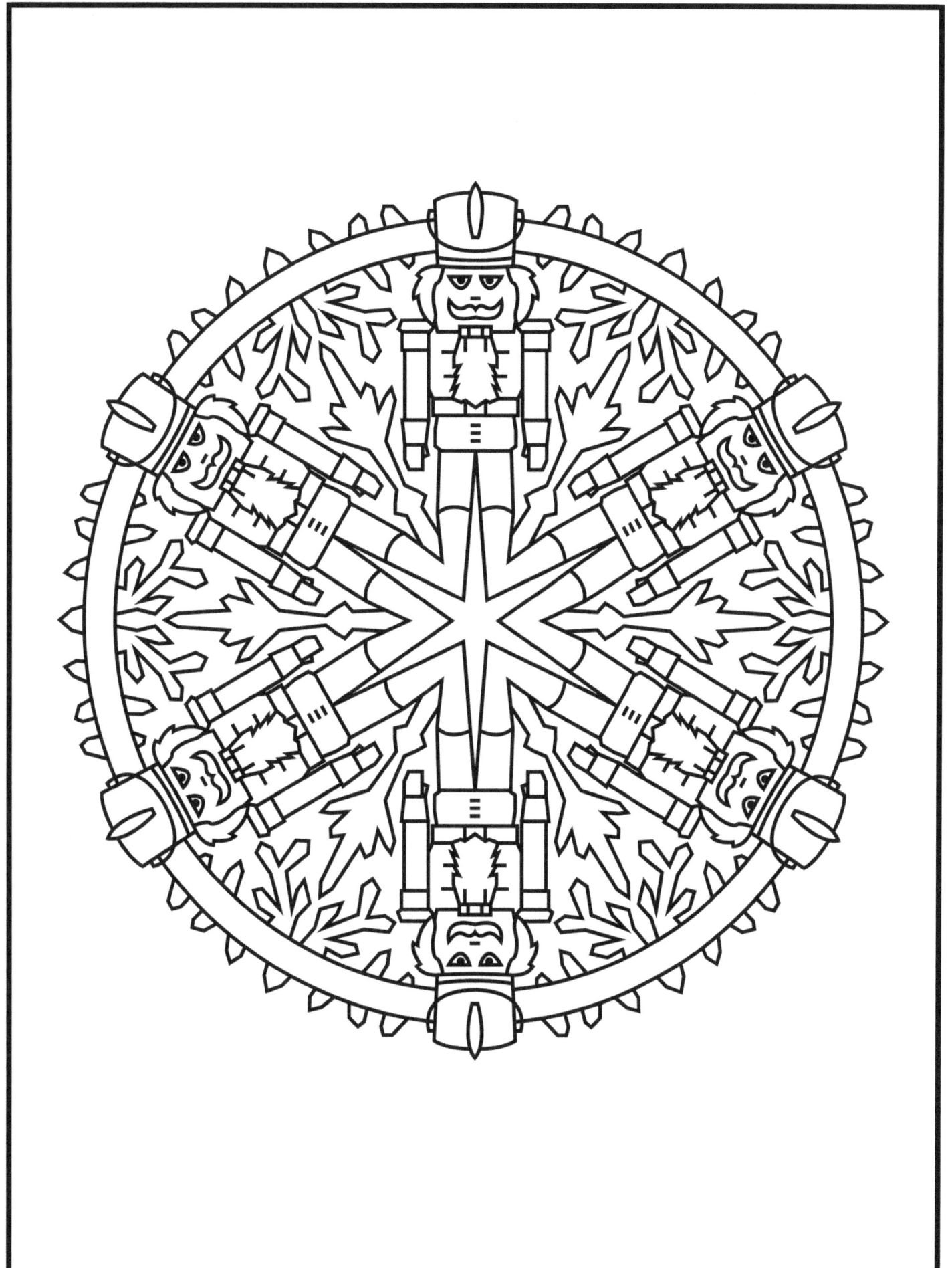

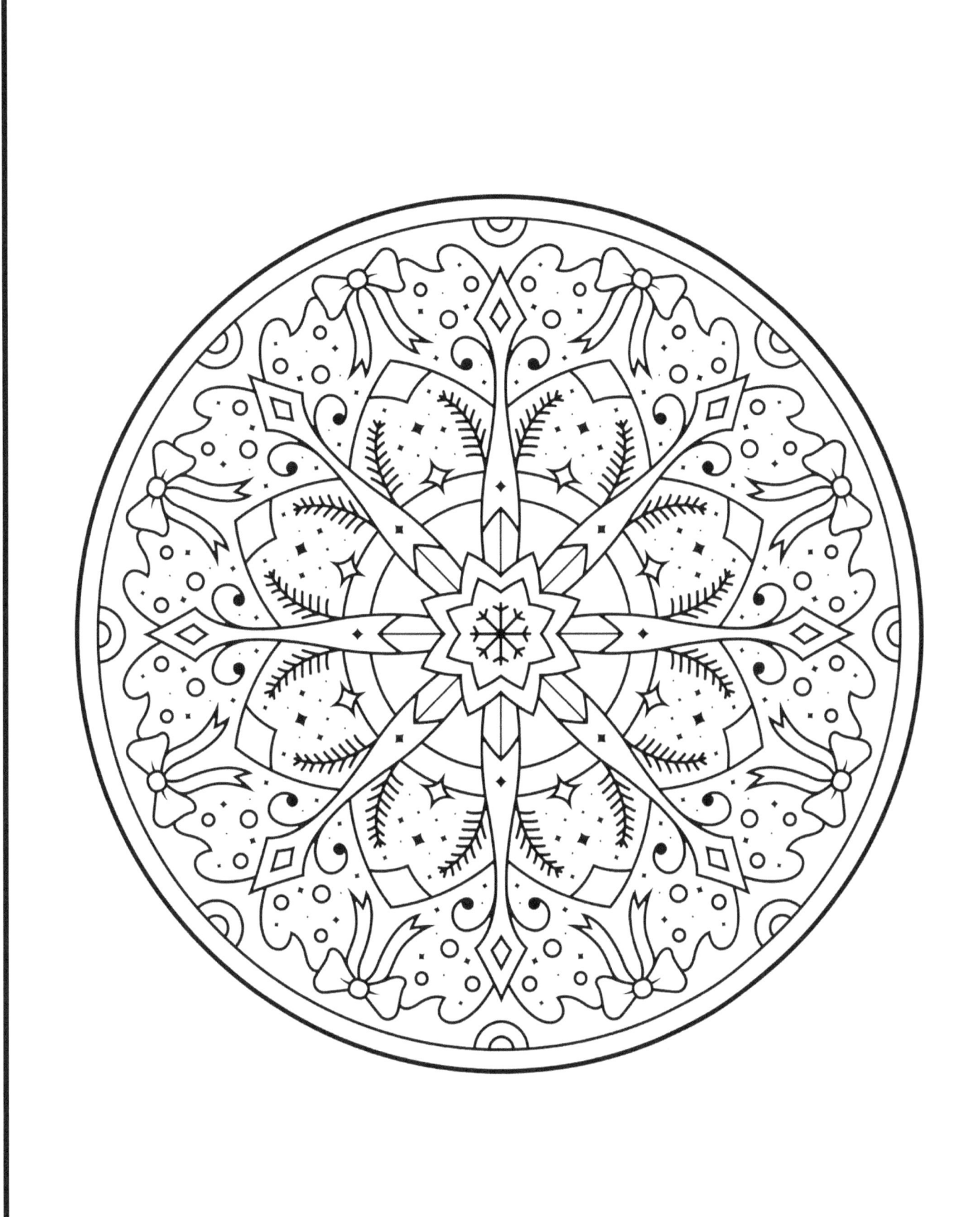

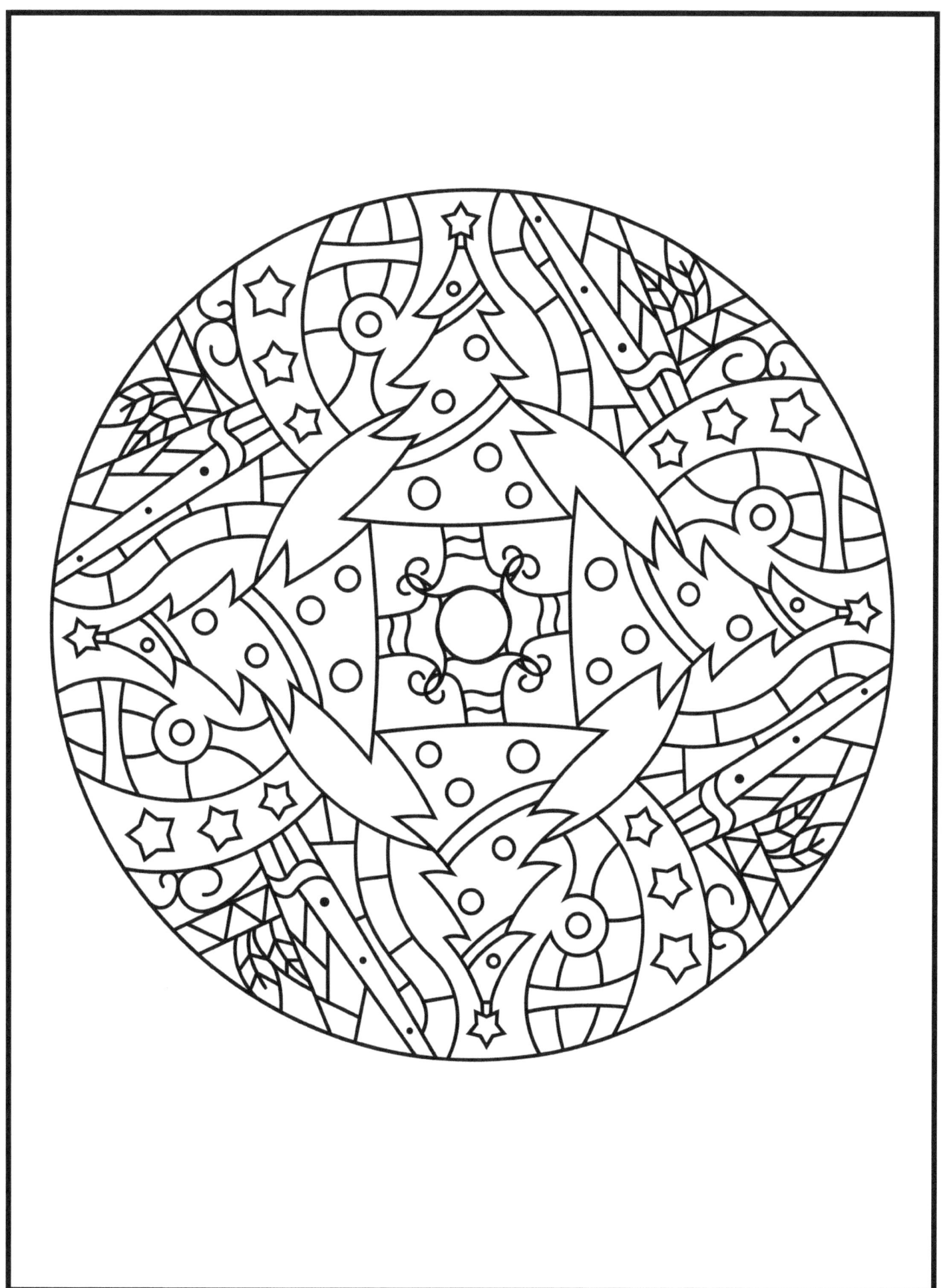

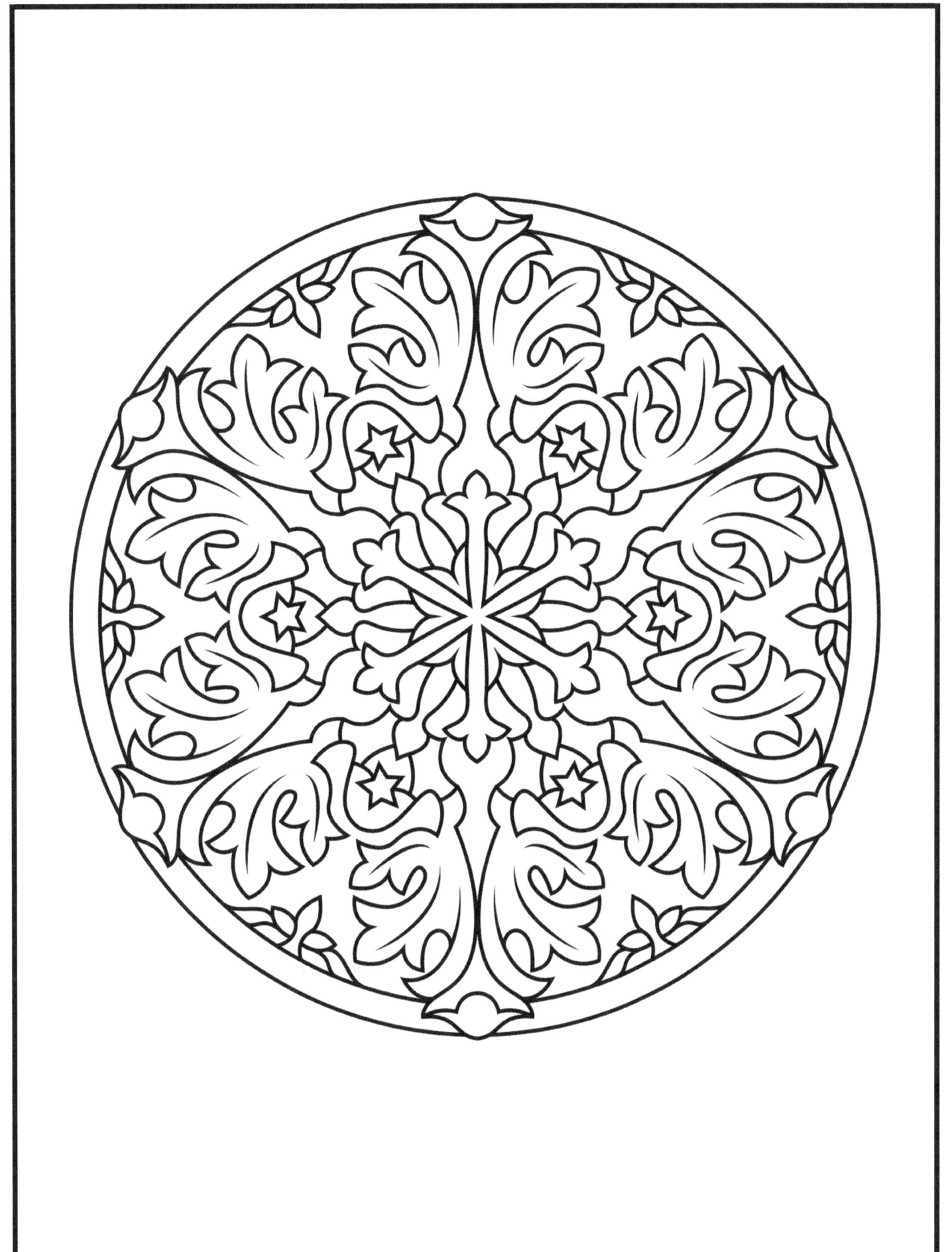

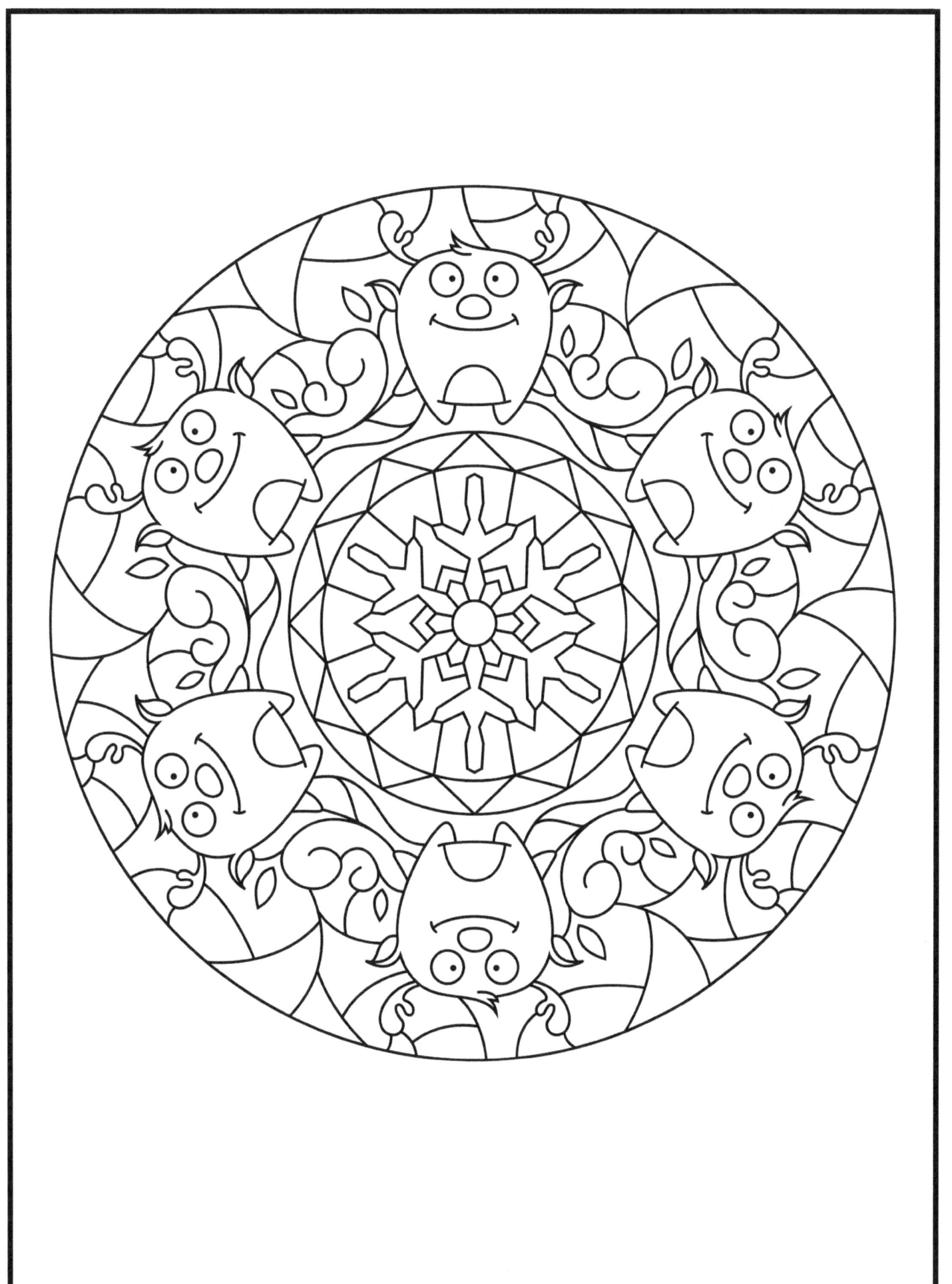

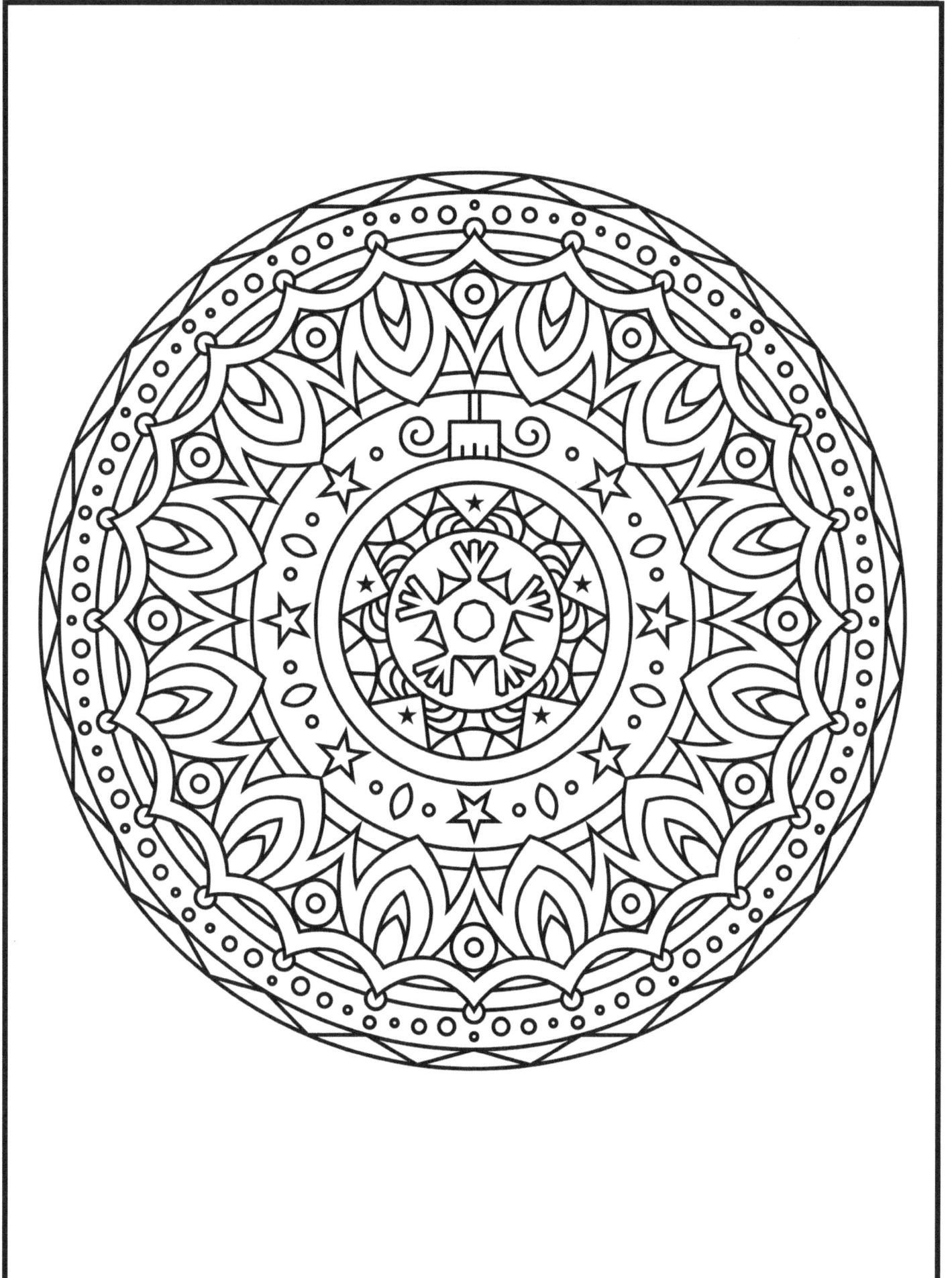

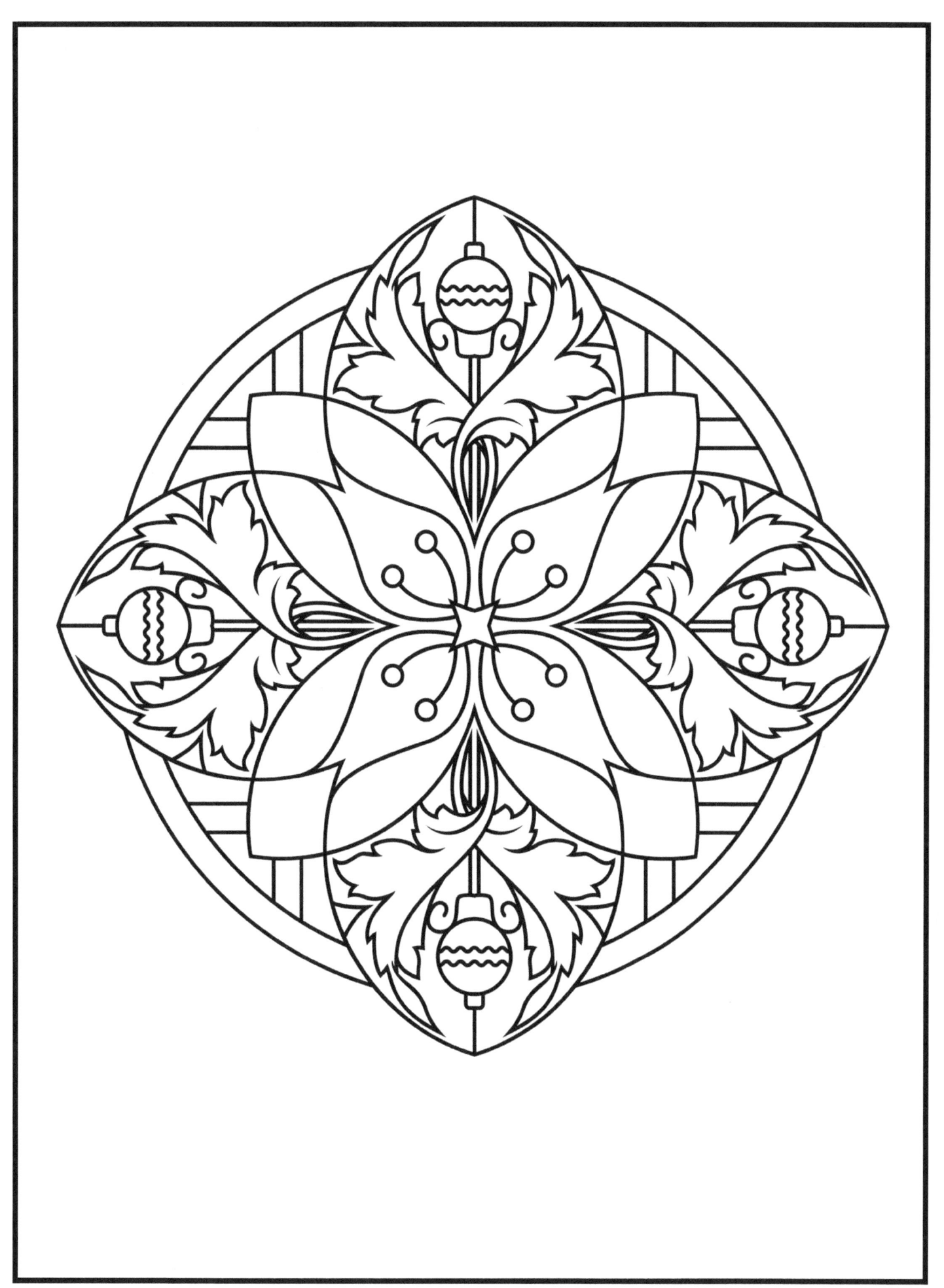

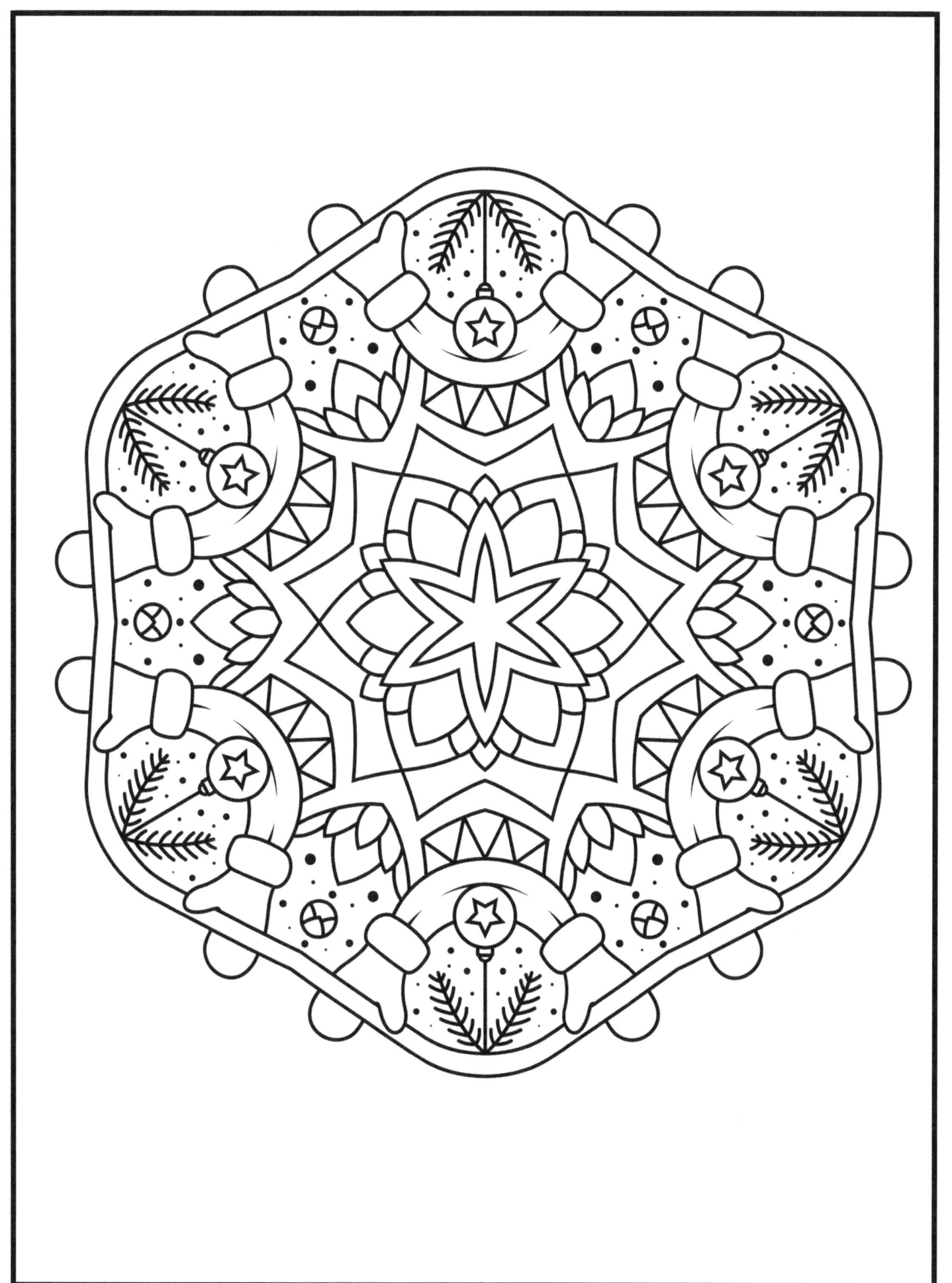

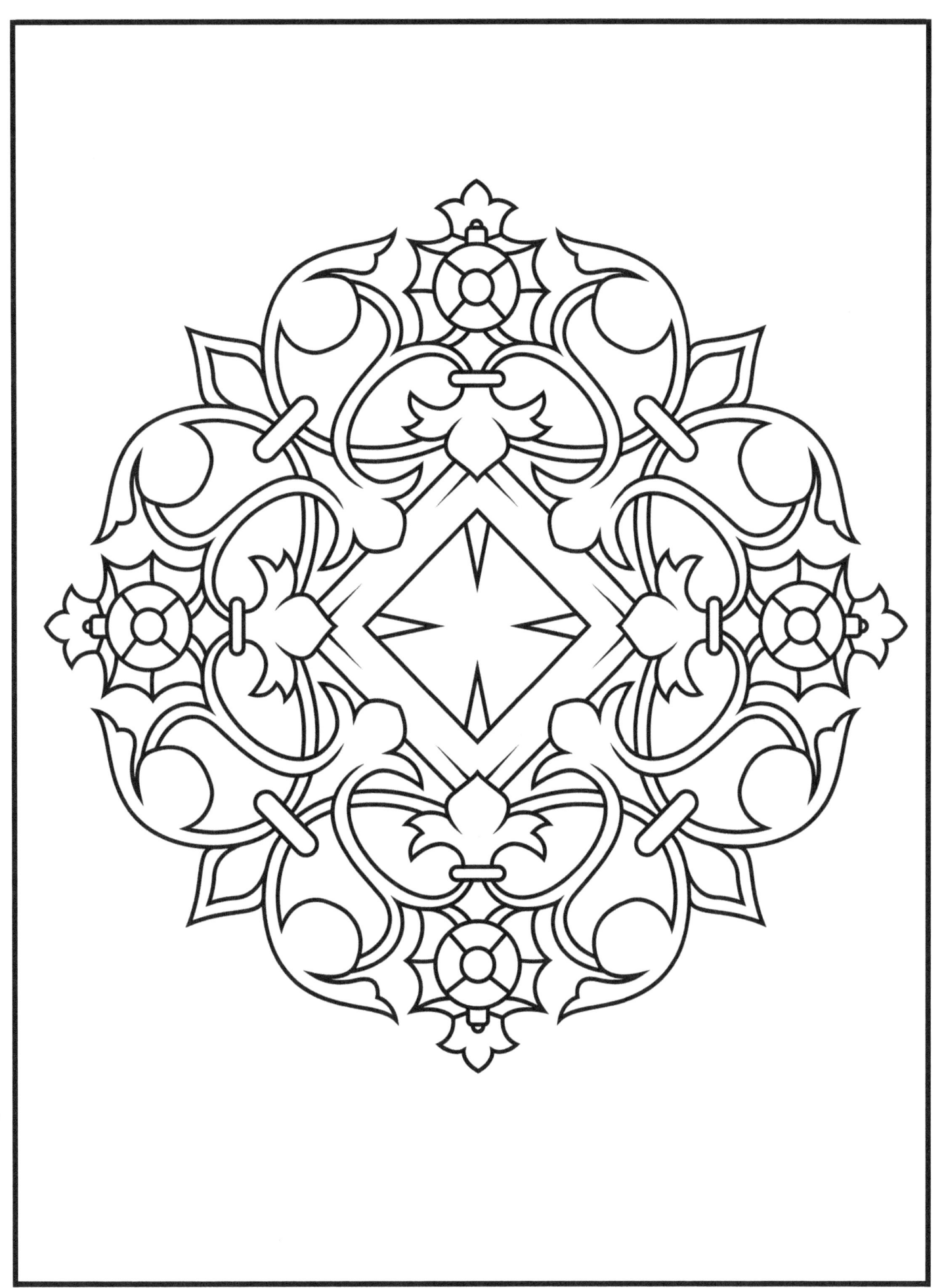

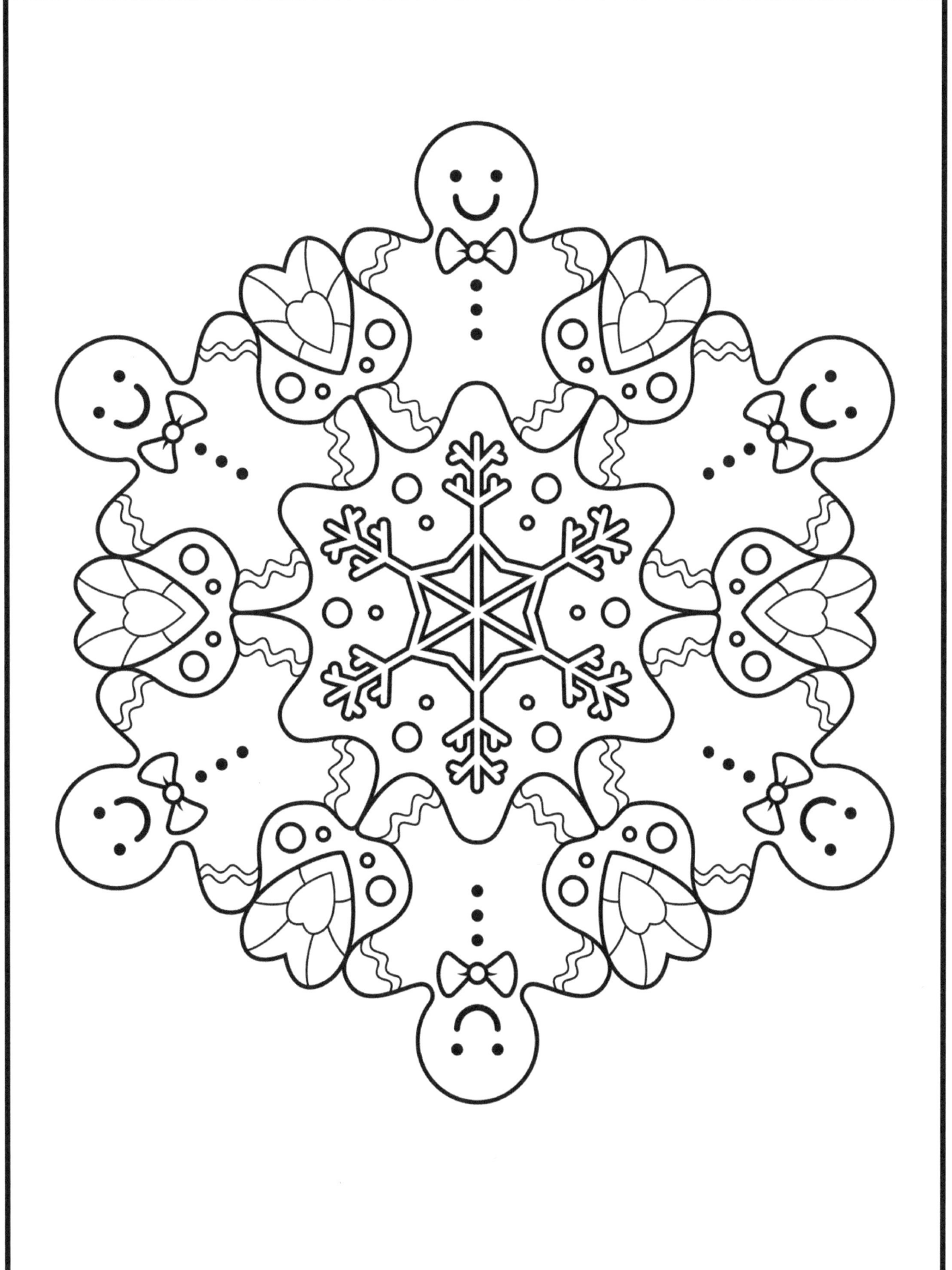

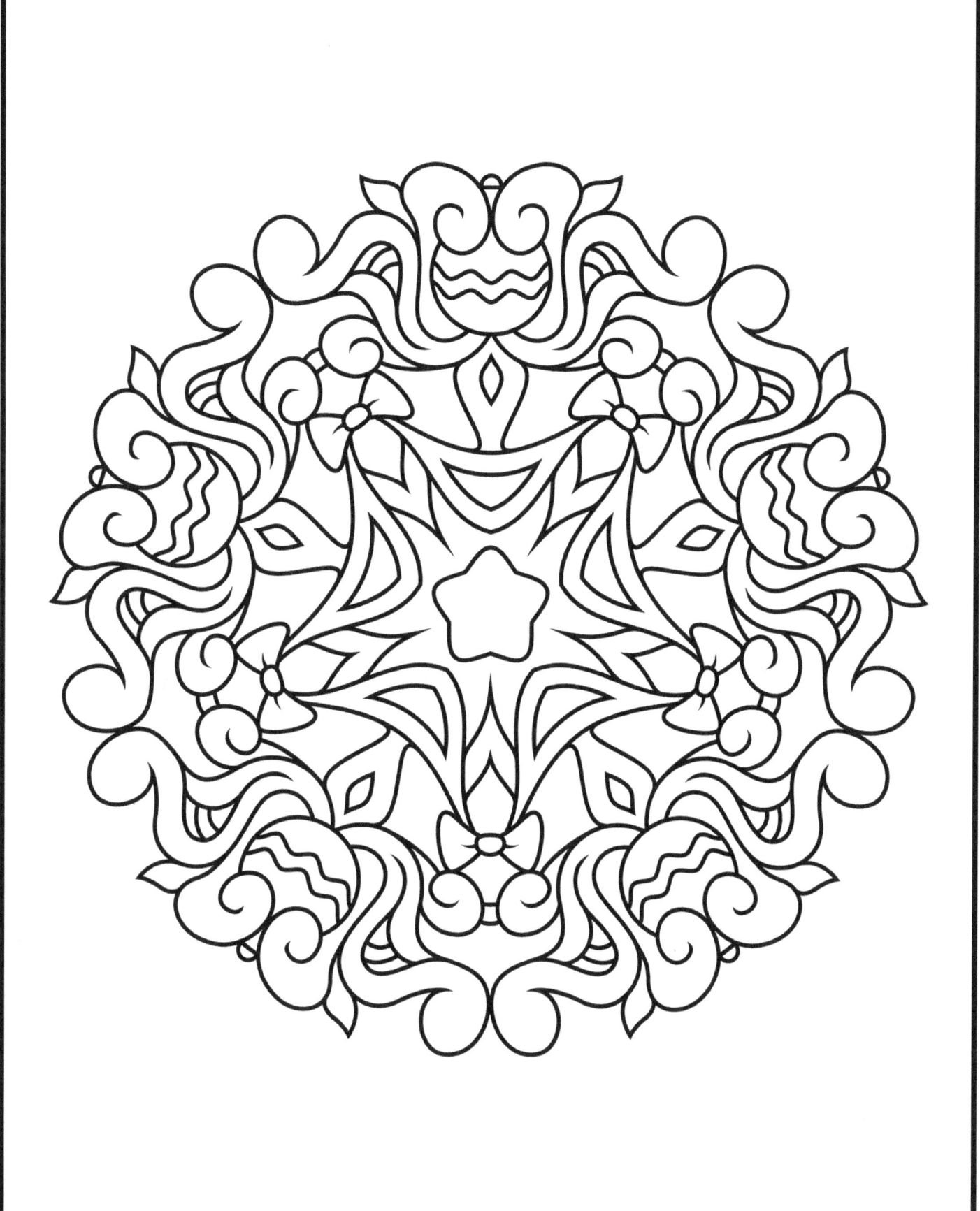

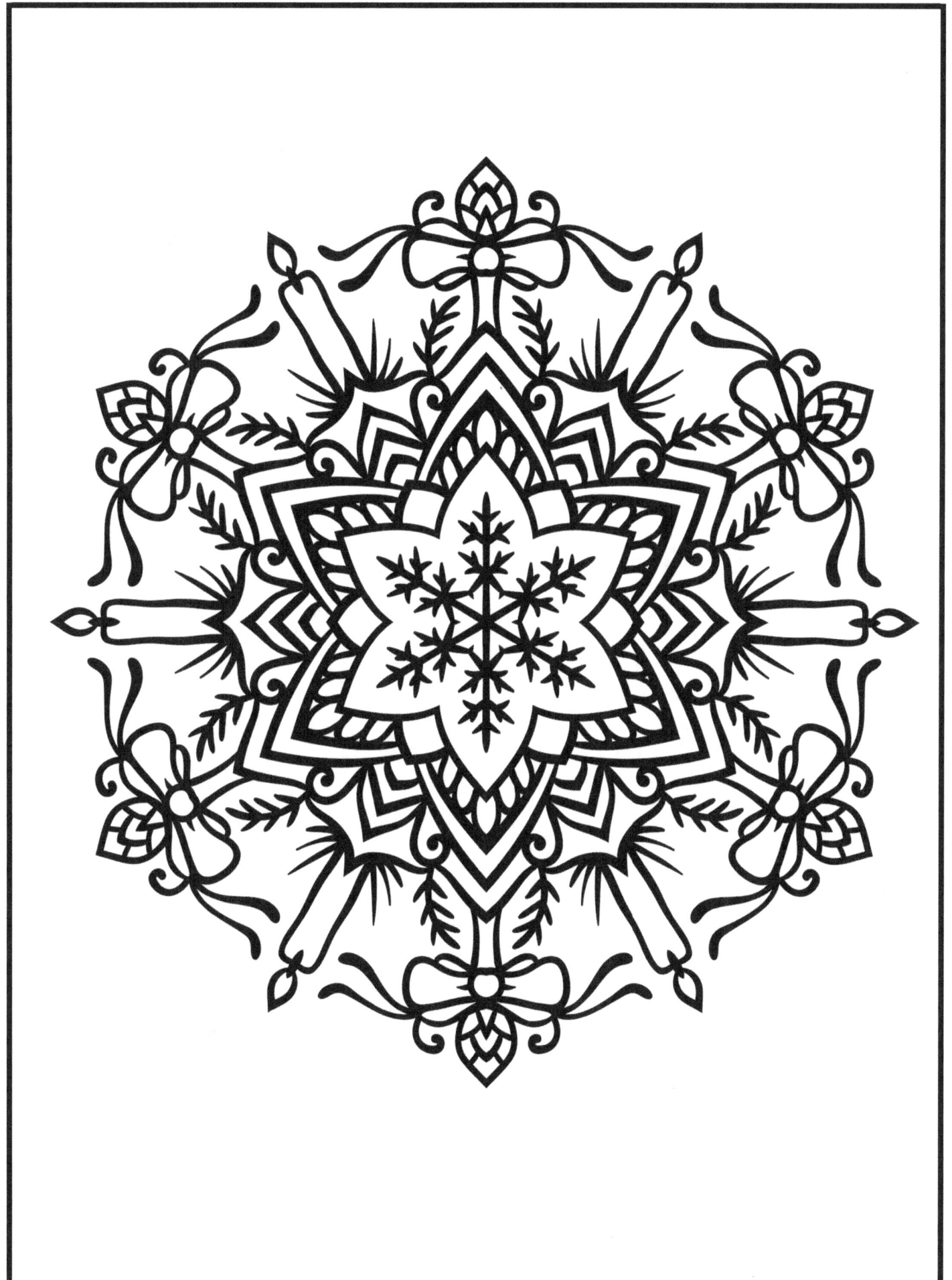

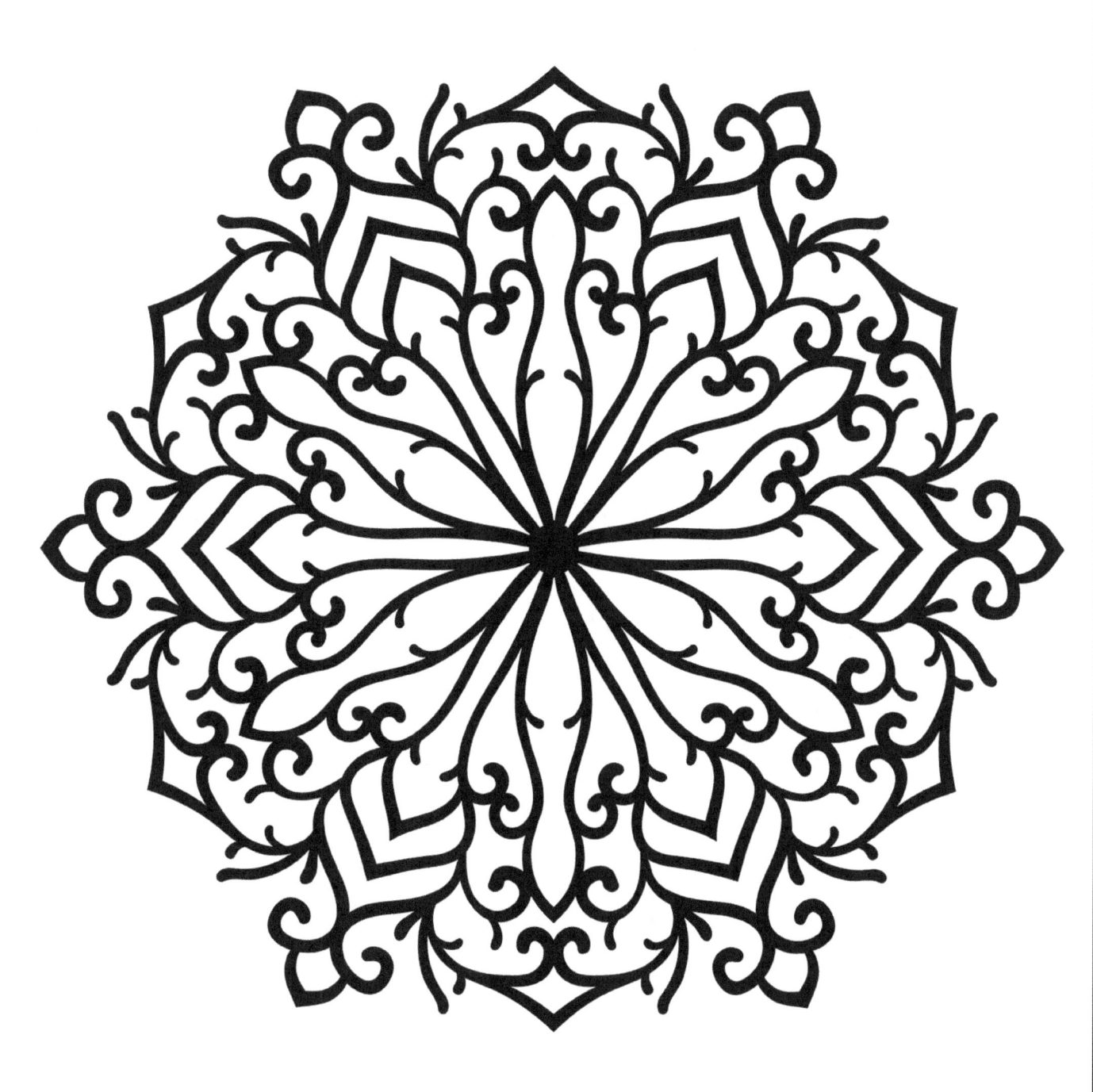

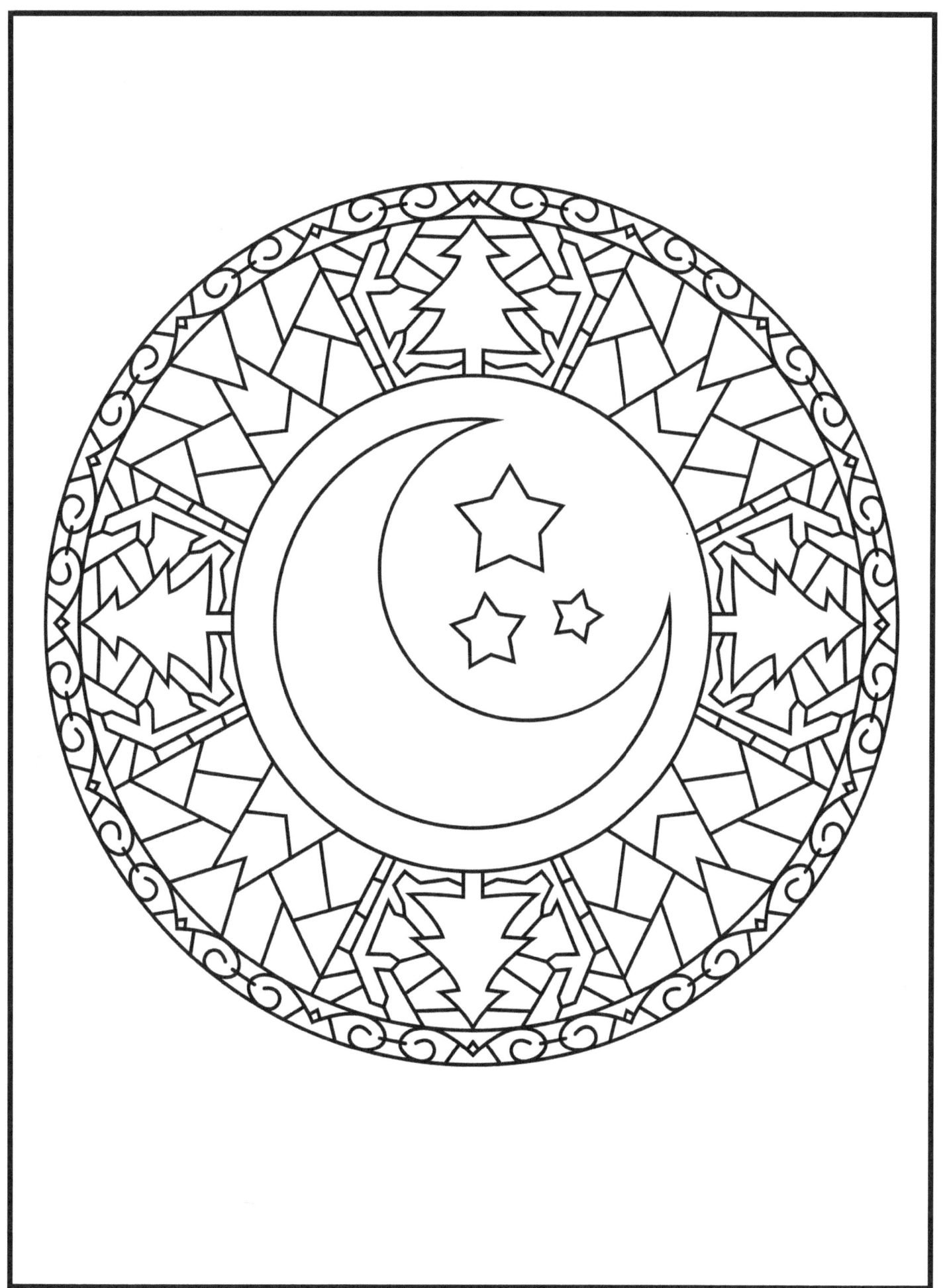

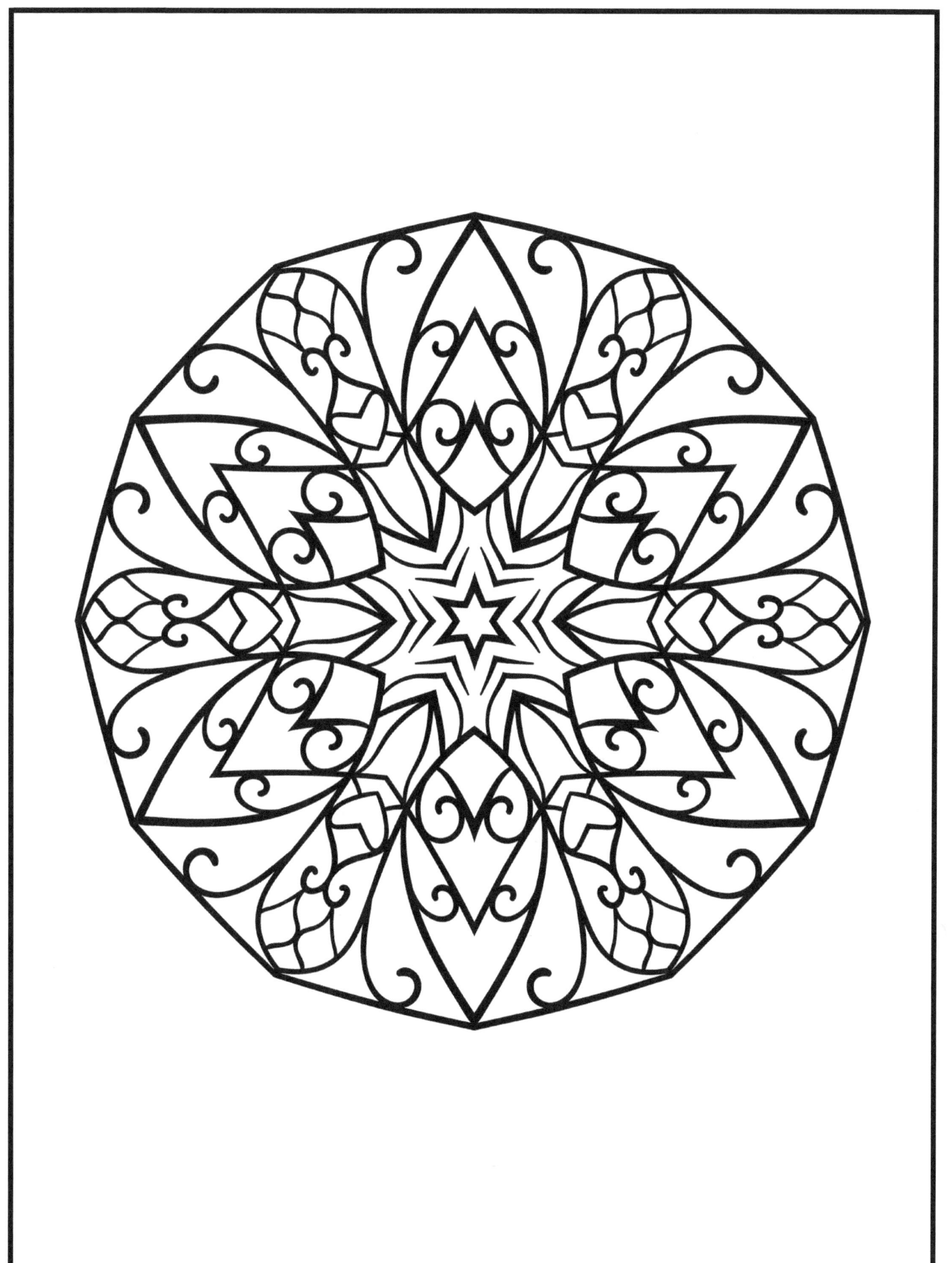

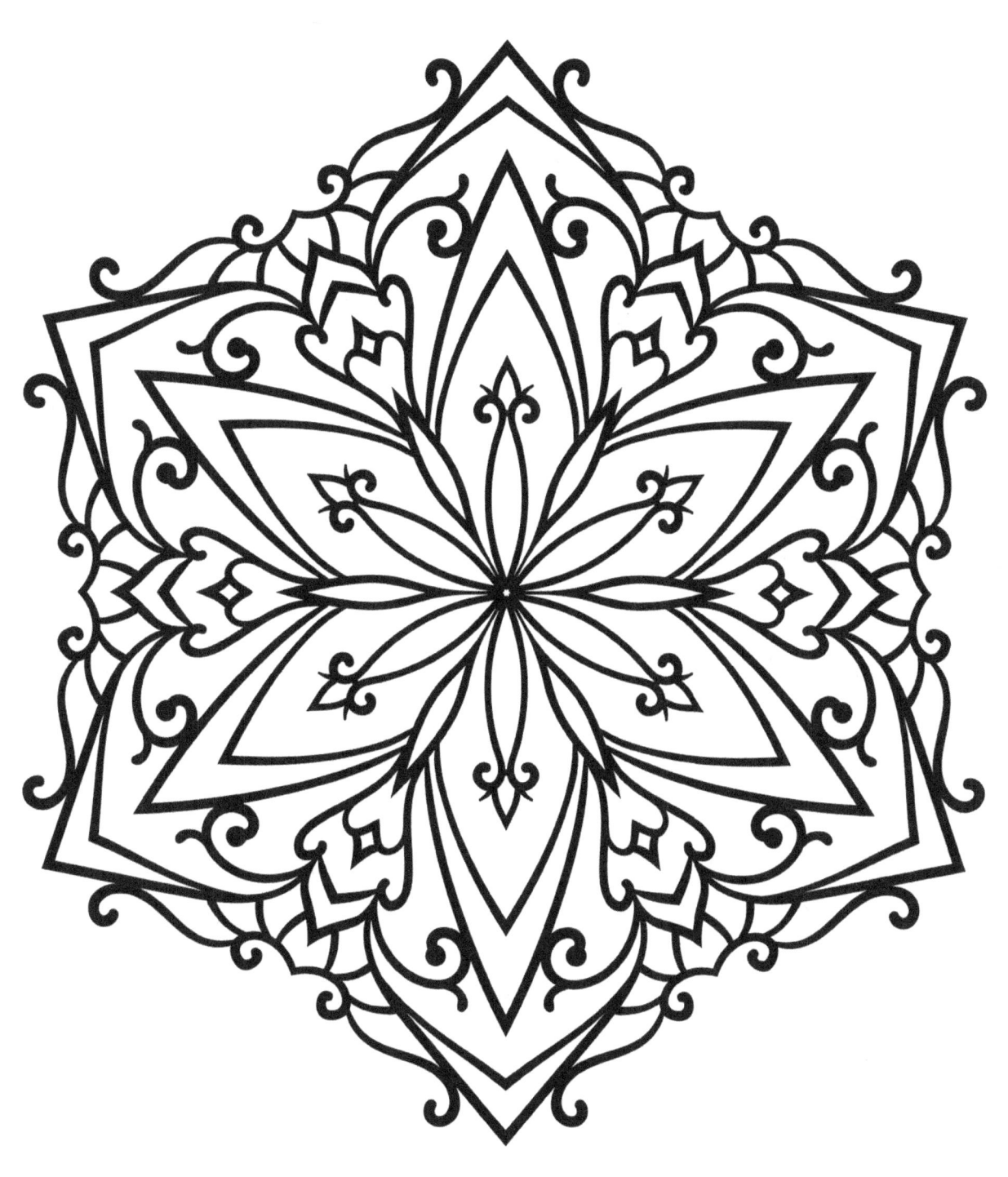

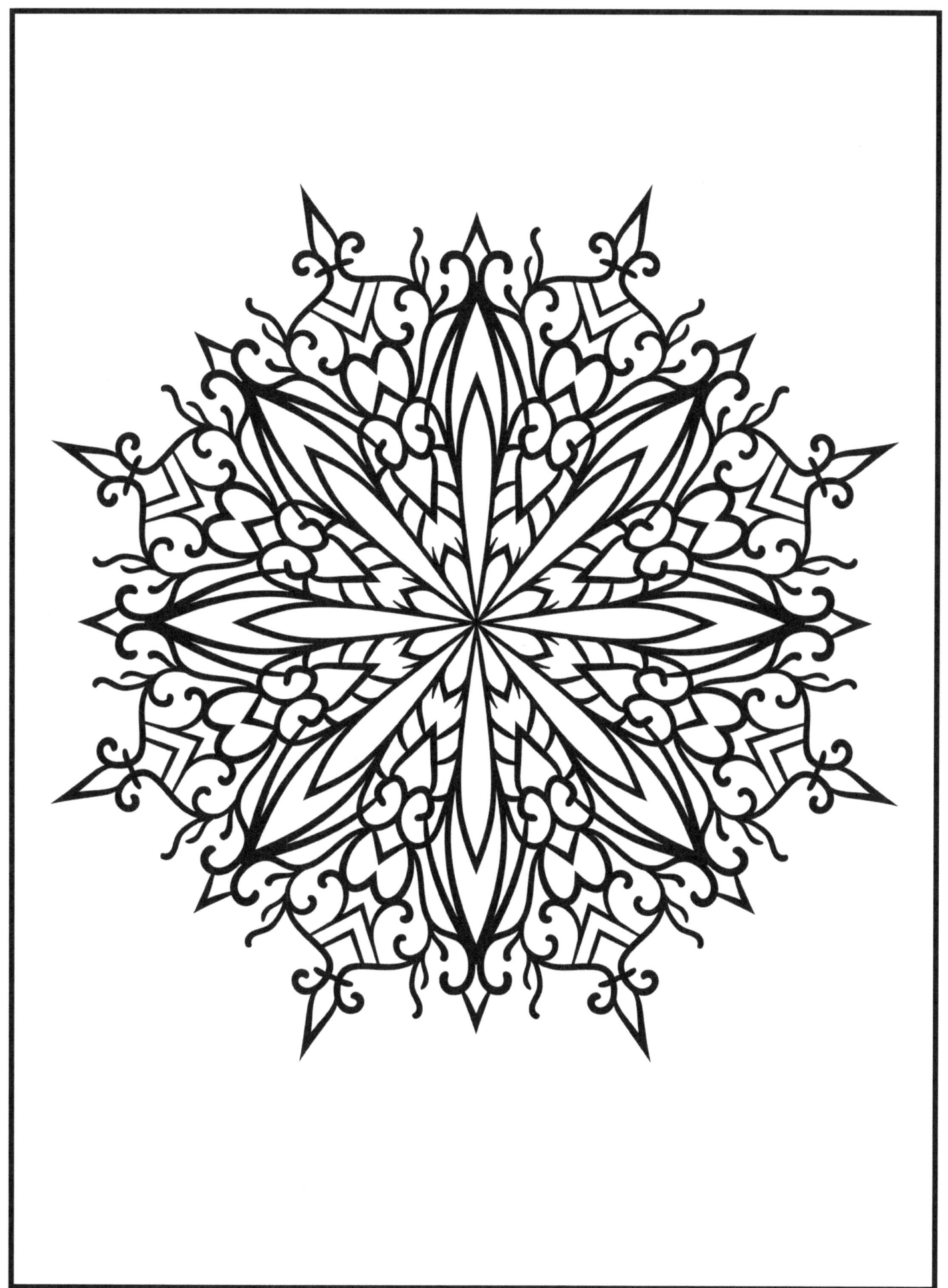

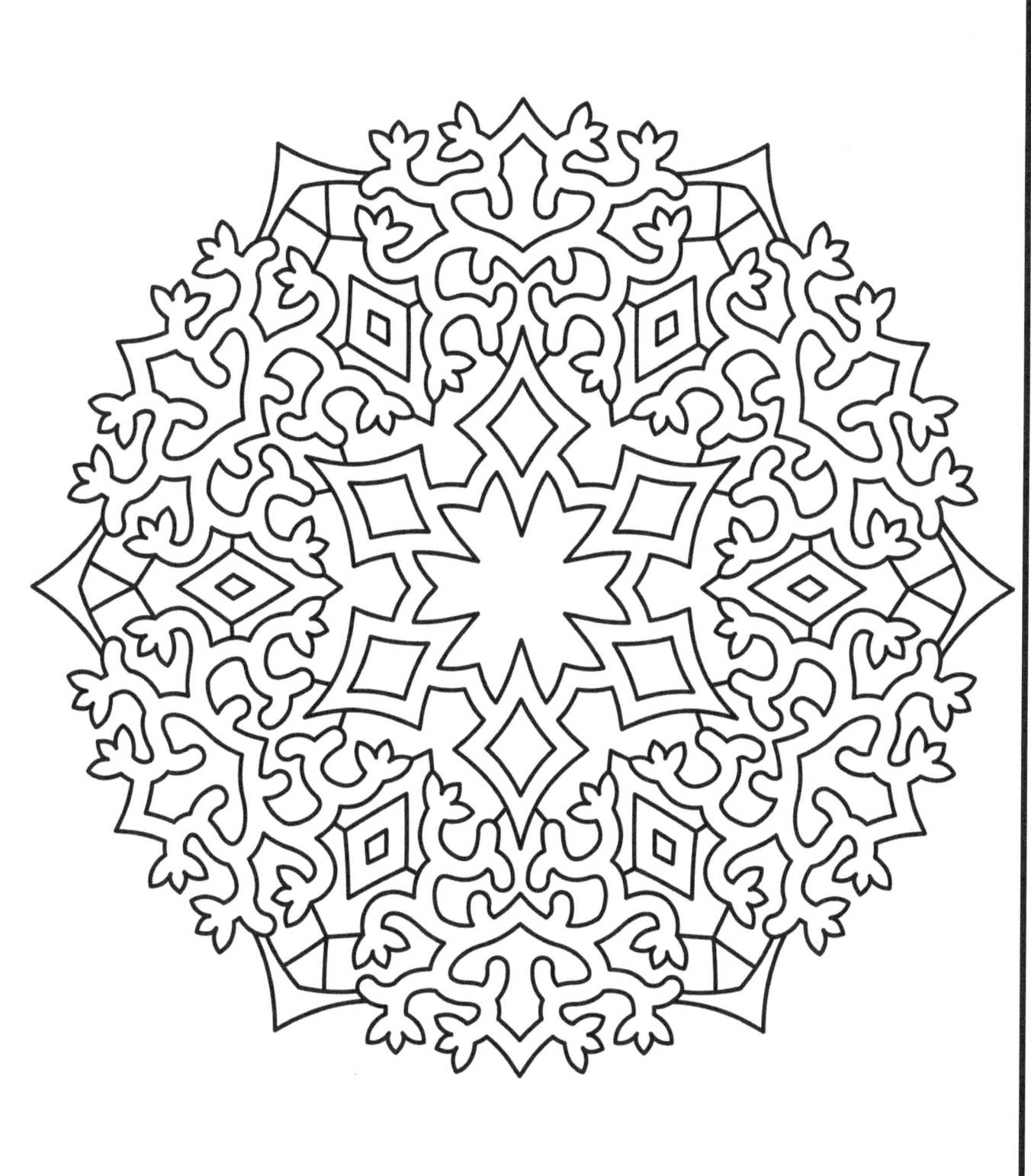

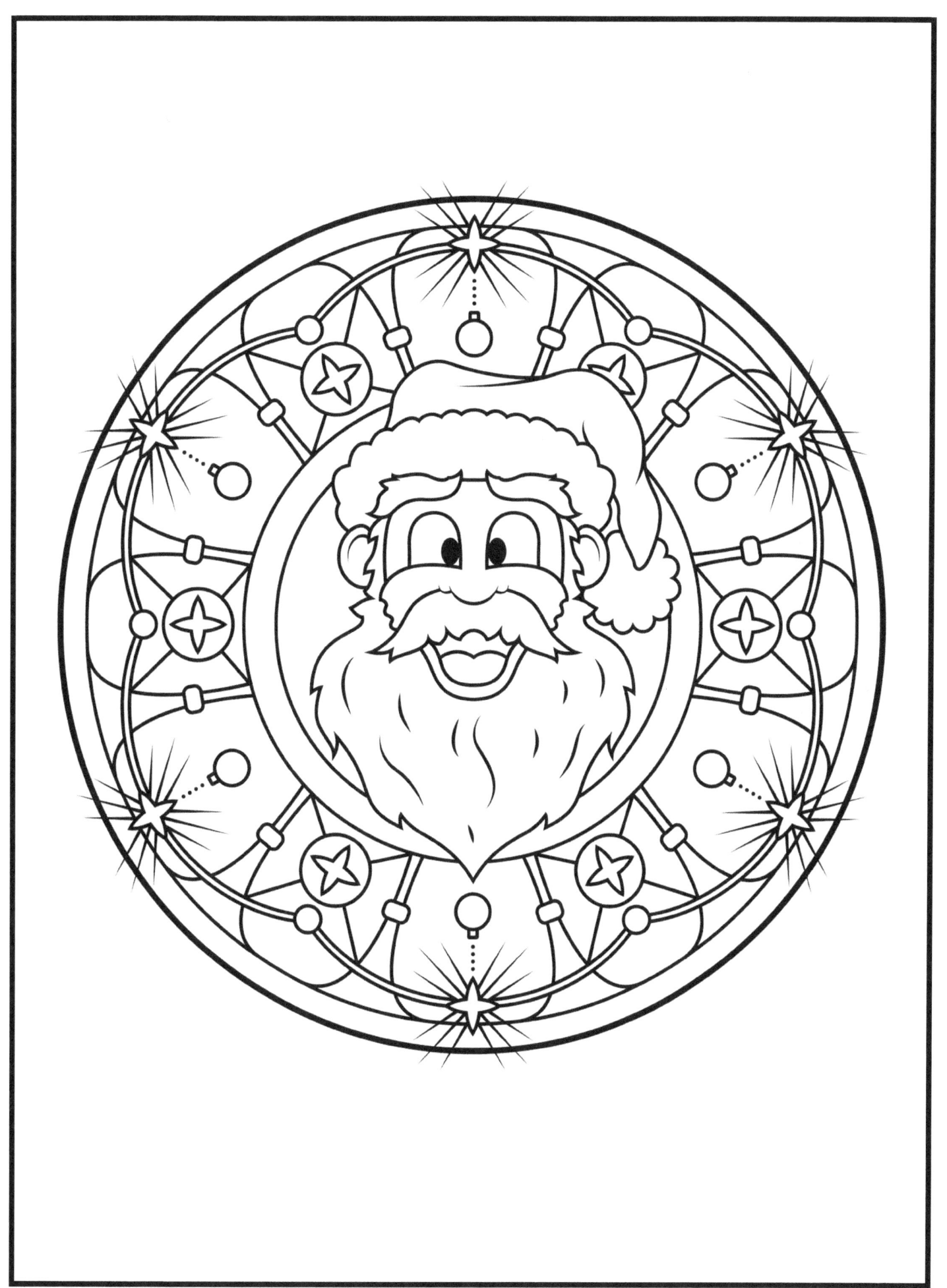

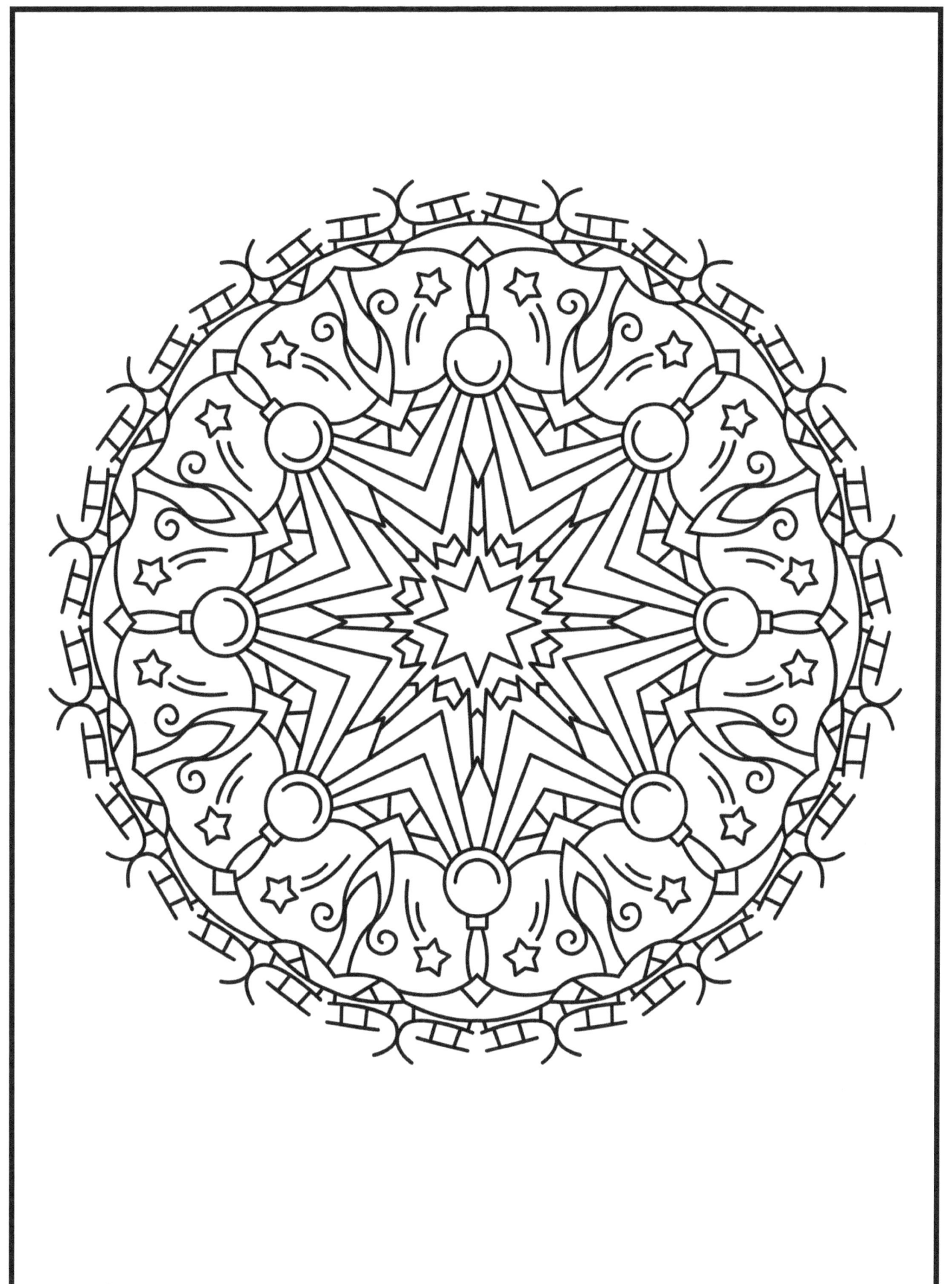

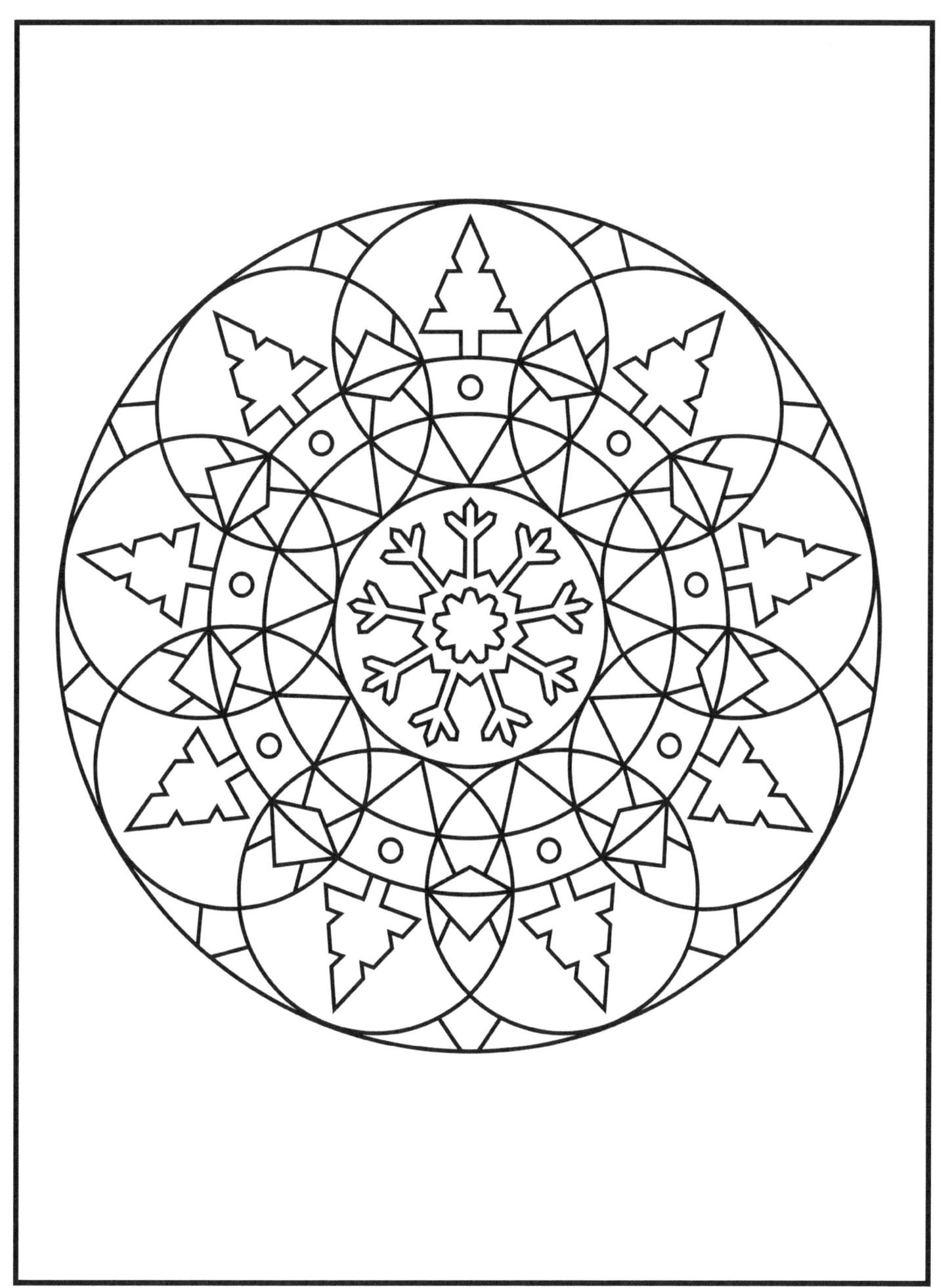

FEATURED

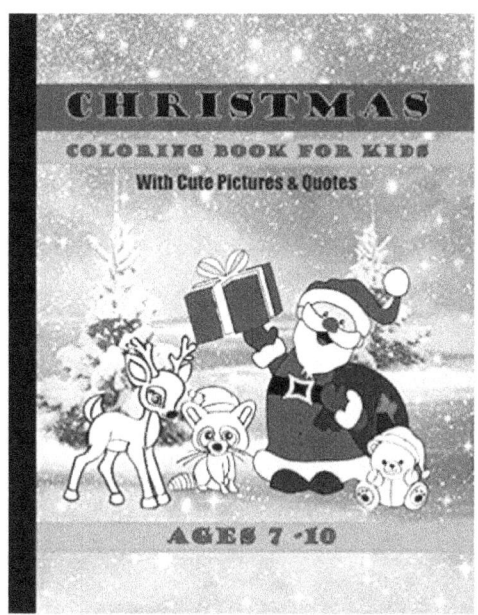 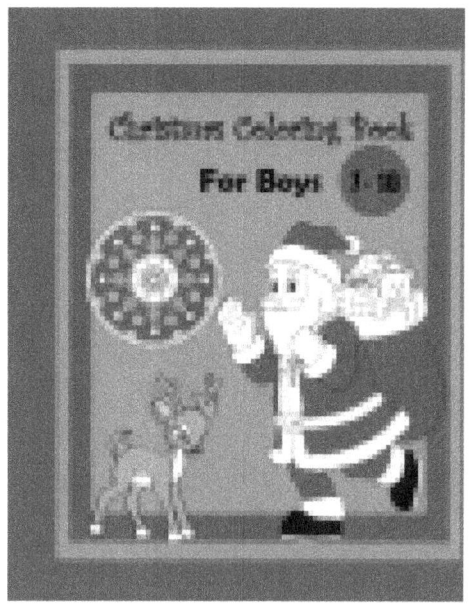

Thank you for your patronage!

Check out cool coloring books, journals, notebooks and planners on our website: www.practicaljournalsandplanners.com

Copyright ©2020 Practical Journals and Planners All rights reserved.
No part of this book may be reproduced or transmitted in any form or by any means electronical or mechanical including photocopying, recording, scanning or any other information storage retrieval system without permission from the Publisher.
www.PracticalJournalsandPlanners.com

www.ingramcontent.com/pod-product-compliance
Lightning Source LLC
Chambersburg PA
CBHW081443220526
45466CB00008B/2489